MILLIE'S SNUGGLY & TOASTY CHRISTMAS

MILLIE'S SNUGGLY & TOASTY CHRISTMAS

MICHAELA TRUEMAN

Silver Devils Publishing

Cover design by Michaela Trueman

First Printing, 2023

Contents

For Sue Baker and Fiona Jenkins, brilliant bookish people.

I

Chapter One

When the doorbell rang, Jude jumped up from the sofa and dashed to answer it, leaving his video game unpaused. 'You're early, not that I'm complaining,' he said as he opened the door.

'Yes, I am. I'm a few weeks early,' replied the woman standing on the drive with two suitcases.

Where Jude had expected to see his fiancée, his sister, Millie, was standing. The sister he thought was in Cambridge.

'What?' Jude questioned.

'I'll explain in a minute. Please may I escape the chilly?' Millie begged.

To prevent his sister from turning into an icicle, Jude replied: 'Yeah, that's cool.'

Upon entering the little mid-terrace her brother called home, Millie felt considerably less cool.

-

Over a mocha and cappuccino, Cecilia and Emma-Leigh chatted about their beloved partners. The friends eventually called it a day so they could get back to the people they'd spent well over an hour talking about.

Once released from the torture of being kept from her partner, Cecilia ran home to him. She hammered on the door, making it quite clear how desperate she was to get inside.

The sight of her partner, complete with his mop of curly brown hair, sent Cecilia's heart rate racing. Before he could say a word, she kissed him, locking her lips with his for quite a few seconds to convey her need.

'Cecilia,' the woman's fiancé moaned.

The way her partner uttered her name told Cecilia, in that moment, he was hers. She could do whatever she wanted to him. As she wanted longer, deeper kisses, and didn't want to freeze, she placed a hand on her partner's chest and encouraged him to retreat into their warm house.

'Cecilia,' her fiancé uttered once more.

Cecilia chuckled and placed her lips on Jude's once more. 'Hush, Jude. Just let me show you how much I love you, unless you object to that,' she whispered as she withdrew.

With a nod to the woman standing in the doorway to the lounge, Jude pointed out: 'My sister might object to that.'

'Millie!' Cecilia cried when she spotted her sister-in-law-to-be.

The feelings which had pestered Cecilia all afternoon finally ceased. They were replaced by the heavy weight of shame.

With a little wave of her hand and a big grin on her face, Millie replied: 'Hi there.'

'Um, sorry. I didn't know you were here,' Cecilia mumbled.

Fits of giggles overcame Millie. When she finally regained her composure, she said: 'Look at your face! I've never seen cheeks so red!'

'Yes, erm, because you caught me kissing your brother, passionately. Sorry,' Cecilia explained.

More laughter erupted from Millie. '"Caught you?" You two are engaged. It's not like it's a shock that you're smooching Jude,' she pointed out.

In response, Cecilia blushed harder.

The silence in the hallway needed sorting. Jude did this by saying: 'Let's go through to the lounge. I bet if we ask nicely, Cecilia will make us cups of tea.'

'Certainly! I'll do it now,' Cecilia agreed, escaping the hallway so swiftly Millie didn't have a chance to tell her how she liked her tea.

To get to the kitchen, Cecilia went through the lounge. Jude and Millie also left the hallway to get to the lounge, but, unlike Cecilia, the siblings remained in the cosy room at the front of the house.

When Millie began to lower herself into the casual grey armchair positioned in the corner of the room by a sleek and stylish tripod lamp, Jude gave her a stern look. The glare prompted her to remember a conversation they'd had five minutes ago about how special the chair was to Cecilia. She shuffled over to the sofa and plonked herself down on it, like Jude had.

Just as Jude had hoped, when Cecilia entered the lounge with cups of tea, her cheeks were their normal colour. She was able to lift her gaze from the floor. The now-composed Cecilia sat in her armchair. Though it was called a coffee table, she was able to place a cup of tea on the piece of furniture next to the chair.

'Why are you here?' Cecilia asked Millie.

'Oh, I missed Jude. I wanted to be home for the holidays,' Millie explained.

The swiftness and breezy tone of Millie's reply caused Cecilia to disregard the words. It was immediately clear she was covering for something.

'But the plan was for you to return to Essex on the twenty-third to stay at the Austen family home. It's only the second today, and this is our home,' Cecilia pointed out.

'But you have a spare room. Surely, I can use it? Please don't send me back!' Millie begged.

Millie wasn't the only Austen pleading with Cecilia. Her brother, Jude, used his eyes to implore Cecilia to give Millie what she wanted. The love she had for her fiancé and his sister overwhelmed the discomfort she felt about having an unexpected guest.

'Calm down, Millie. It is late in the day. You may stay the night here, with us,' Cecilia assured her.

An audible sigh escaped Millie. 'Thanks. You are the best sister-in-law a girl could wish for,' she told Cecilia.

To emphasise her point, Millie jumped off the sofa, dashed over to Cecilia, bent over, and hugged her.

Whilst being hugged, Cecilia thought: '*Even in this awkward position, she gives good hugs.*'

When it felt like she'd held Cecilia oddly for long enough, Millie returned to the sofa and Jude. As she sat down, she stroked the fabric with her hands.

'So, Millie, how have you been?' Cecilia asked.

'Uni is *snazzy*! My subject is fascinating. It is in fact so fascinating that it's hard for me to not go on and on about it. I restrain myself though because, as I've been told many times, no-one but me cares about dead thinky people. Cambridge itself is as beauteous as ever. I'm a very lucky girl,' Millie enthused.

'That all sounds... good,' Jude commented.

'It is. So, tell me about you. What's been going on?' Millie replied.

'But, don't you have more to tell us?' Jude questioned.

Millie shook her head emphatically. 'Absolutely not. There's nothing more I can say. Please, coupley people, fill me in on your lives,' she said.

Even though they hadn't told each other so in words, Jude and Cecilia knew they'd both much rather hear how Millie had been than talk about themselves. They also silently agreed Millie was unwilling to talk about her own life, so they should distract her with tales of their own.

'We've been planning bits for the wedding,' Cecilia told Millie.

Jude snorted. 'What Cecilia means is, *she's* been planning things for it. I don't get no say in anything,' he corrected.

This made them all laugh. On the surface, Millie's unspoken problems were forgotten. Inside, all three of them were thinking about what was wrong with the girl. It took effort to maintain a conversation about venues and catering, but they did it to avoid the hidden depths of whatever had inspired Millie to flee home weeks earlier than planned.

2

Chapter Two

A kiss on his shoulder surprised Jude. He and Cecilia had undressed and slipped into bed in silence. This had led him to believe she was cross with him because his sister had turned up unannounced and he'd let her stay, so he'd turned his back on Cecilia.

'We'll help her. We'll get to the bottom of this. Don't worry, Jude,' Cecilia whispered.

From the moment Millie had turned up on the doorstep, Jude had felt alone. The soft and supportive words from his fiancée reminded him that wasn't the case. Cecilia wasn't cross at all. She cared just as much as he did. Had he not have been so blinded by panic and a general feeling of inadequacy, Jude would have known Cecilia was supportive. Her warm and caring nature was part of what he loved about her.

'What the hell happened in Cambridge? Why can't I get it out of her? She needs me, that much is clear, and I've failed her,' Jude wondered out loud.

Cecilia shuffled closer and put an arm around Jude. He could feel the comforting warmth of her naked body against his. It soothed his troubled soul.

'Hush, Jude. Don't talk like that. She's here, safe with us. You haven't failed her at all. You're a most wonderful brother, and together we'll help her. We already *are* helping her,' Cecilia told him.

Tears threatened to escape Jude. 'But what can we do? This is your home. I can't expect you to put her up here for more than a few nights,' he questioned.

With the arm she'd wrapped around him, Cecilia squeezed Jude tight against her. 'Not *my* home, *our* home. You're my future spouse. Millie will be my sister-in-law one day. I want to look after her as much as you do. What we can do is be there for her. If that means her staying here, so be it,' she replied.

~

The warm cuddle was the only communication between Jude and Cecilia for a while. Though it was silent outside it, Jude's head buzzed with theories about what may have upset Millie, and questions about what to do for her.

When almost an hour had passed, Cecilia sighed and rolled away from Jude. It didn't surprise him. The central heating had kicked in and the room was warming up. Cuddling wasn't as comfortable as it had been.

A few moments after she'd turned over, Cecilia flicked the bedside lamp on. Its energy saving bulb emitted a gentle glow that increased gradually.

'Would you like a cup of tea? I'm going to get up for a minute,' Cecilia offered.

'Nah, thanks. Are you just getting up to make tea, cos I could make it for you? Save you having to leave your nice, warm bed,' Jude asked.

After sitting up and swinging her legs over the edge of the

bed, Cecilia explained: 'Thank you, but please don't. I'm getting up because I can't sleep.'

'Ah, yeah! You ain't supposed to just toss and turn all night, are you? Getting up is meant to help,' Jude realised.

'I think so. Opinions differ on that, but I don't feel laying in bed with my mind ticking is helpful,' Cecilia confirmed.

When Cecilia stood, her naked body was backlit by the lamp. It didn't escape her notice that Jude took the opportunity to admire her beauty. His eyes clearly scanned her.

'Beautiful woman,' Jude murmured.

With her confidence boosted by her partner's open admiration of her naked form, Cecilia almost skipped across the room to retrieve her dressing gown from the hook it hung on by the door. The heavy softness of it comforted her when she wrapped it round herself.

As she slipped out the bedroom door, Cecilia whispered to Jude: 'I'll just be a minute.'

Having lived in the house for years, Cecilia could easily navigate the stairs in the dark. The cold, smooth wood of the continuous handrail guided her down to the hallway. Clouds concealed the moon and the streetlights had been turned off for an hour, so no light crept around the curtains. To banish the darkness, Cecilia flicked the lounge light on. The room was instantly flooded with brilliant white light, temporarily blinding her.

Once she was able to see, Cecilia tiptoed through the lounge to the kitchen. As it was an inanimate object and no-one else had made tea, the kettle was just where she'd left it. That made it easy for her to locate it and put it on to boil. In the quiet of the night, the noise the kettle made as it heated water to 100 degrees Celsius seemed deafening. Cecilia was simultaneously aware of being alone on the ground floor and of the presence of people on the first floor who could be disturbed by the noise. It was unnerving.

-

Above Cecilia, Jude was laying in bed. Despite being aware of NHS guidance that advised against looking at your phone when you were trying to get to sleep for various reasons, he was scrolling through his emails, deleting some of the many sales messages that bombarded his inbox every day. It didn't do its job of distracting him from his anxiety about Millie. The tearful feeling he had didn't go away. Some water escaped his eyes. Jude made no attempt to stop the silent tears. There was no reason to hide how distressed he was.

When he stumbled across a three-year-old email containing a code for a click and collect order that had been forwarded to him, Jude's tears dried on their own. Though he still didn't know what had happened to Millie in Cambridge, he now knew where she could stay in Colchester whilst he tried to work out what the problem was.

-

Jude wasn't the only Austen in the house who was crying. In the little spare bedroom, Millie was sobbing into her pillow. It was normal to her now, so she barely noticed. Silent tears were part of her bedtime routine.

3

Chapter Three

Like they had for a week, the glossy white cupboard doors shone under weak sunlight just about getting through the window. The sink above them was empty, so it was possible to see it was sparkling too. It had taken someone a lot of work to keep the kitchen in that state. The person who'd put all that work in took a moment to appreciate the result of it before he undid it by making himself a hot chocolate.

A phone call to the man's mobile postponed the making of hot chocolate, which gave the kitchen a few more minutes of spotlessness. 'Hey, Floyd. You got a minute?' the caller asked.

For Jude, the man who'd called, Floyd always had a minute. He did in fact have several minutes for Jude. To let his friend know this, Floyd replied: 'Yeah, sure.'

'I just wanted to ask if you'd replaced that housemate of yours yet,' Jude revealed.

'No, I haven't got round to it. I can afford a few months without a housemate, especially as I'm single so don't have a girl to treat, but

I ought to get onto it. Right now I'm just enjoying having a quiet, clean house,' Floyd told Jude.

When Jude didn't immediately answer, Floyd realised he'd called to ask a favour. A sense of dread overwhelmed him. He expressed his anxiety by saying: 'Please tell me you and Cecilia haven't had a row. I mean, you're welcome if you have, but I'd be gutted. I thought Cecilia was The One for you.'

'What? Oh, nah, don't worry. Me and Cecilia are good. It ain't me who needs a place to stay,' Jude assured Floyd.

Though the fears about his friend's relationship had been allayed, Floyd felt too tired to stand. This was due to the fact he'd stayed up until one in the morning to shave a few seconds off his best lap time at Rainbow Road on his favourite video game. He'd achieved his goal, but had done so at the expense of a good night's sleep.

There was nowhere to sit in the kitchen, so Floyd wandered through to the lounge. He sat down on the sofa to take the weight off his tired feet. 'Who is it that you want to be my new housemate?' Floyd asked once he was comfortable.

'My little sister. She's back from Cambridge for Christmas and needs somewhere to be. Cecilia and I would pay you for the month, so that'd sort the money thing,' Jude revealed.

'Oh, Millie? I've never met her, but I've always wanted to,' Floyd replied.

'Well, do you wanna live with her for a month and a bit then, as long as she wants to too? You'd know her very well by the end,' Jude asked.

When Jude talked about his sister, it was always with great affection. The siblings were quite close.

When Jude had been Floyd's housemate, it had been a great arrangement. The two young men had been quite close.

It didn't take long for Floyd to make his decision. Three seconds after Jude had asked him if he wanted to live with Millie, Floyd replied: 'Yeah, let's do this.'

4

Chapter Four

Partly because she was dreading facing Jude and Cecilia, and partly because the bed was comfy, Millie remained in the spare bedroom until almost ten in the morning. When she ventured downstairs, she found Cecilia in the kitchen at the dining table, laptop open in front of her.

'Good morning, I'm sorry...' Millie began. When Cecilia held a hand up, she stopped.

'No, I'm the one who's sorry. Whatever it was you were about to say will have to wait twenty minutes. I'm in the middle of something,' Cecilia replied.

As Cecilia continued to focus on her screen, Millie shuffled out of the room to leave her to it. Without giving it much thought, she sank down onto the sofa. There was no sign of Jude. She assumed he must have had to go to work.

To occupy herself, Millie admired her surroundings. She snapped a picture and sent it to Maddie, a friend and housemate from uni.

Before Millie had even locked her phone, a reply from Maddie came. "Beautiful! Is this your brother's place?" it read.

As she knew Maddie quite well, Millie heard her voice when she read the message. She knew it would confuse her that Jude had such a smart home. Millie's fingers glided across the keyboard on her phone to explain why Jude's house didn't look like Maddie expected it to.

"It's his gorilla's place. She seemed it" Millie sent to Maddie.

A few seconds later, Millie received a picture of Maddie with her hand on her chin and a furrowed brow. Clearly, her friend was confused. That confused Millie. She understood the picture was a real-life representation of an emoji, for the friends always replaced emojis with expressive pictures of themselves, but Millie's message had been perfectly clear.

When Millie reread her message, she saw her mistake. To Maddie she wrote: "Wondered why you were confuzzled for a moment there. I meant his GIRLFRIEND'S place, which she DECORATED. Damn Swipy typing."

Whilst waiting for Maddie to answer, Millie longed to be in Cambridge with her. Remembering Maddie had left Cambridge for the holidays but someone else had remained in their student house quelled that wish.

"Ah, that's fair" Maddie sent to Millie.

To keep the conversation going, Millie wanted to reply to Maddie. Unfortunately for her, she couldn't think of a response to "Ah, that's fair". This meant she couldn't chat to Maddie anymore.

When her phone buzzed to inform her of another message from Maddie, Millie almost leapt off the sofa in delight. Reading the message made her even happier. It said: "Miss you gorgeous girl."

'Miss you too, Maddie,' Millie whispered to her phone.

After saying it out loud, Millie typed her message to her friend. As she sent it, she heard Cecilia shut her laptop.

A few seconds later, Cecilia entered the room. Her blue gaze felt cold to Millie and made her shiver. Millie was very pleased when Cecilia sat in the armchair rather than next to her on the sofa.

'How are you this morning, Millie?' Cecilia asked.

'Erm, fine,' Millie replied.

'Is there anything I can do for you?' Cecilia enquired.

'No, no, thank you. I feel uncomfy enough about trespassing in your home, thank you,' Millie stammered.

A second after she'd spoken, Millie realised her words could be misinterpreted. 'Not that your home is uncomfy. It's beauteous, thank you. Please don't send me home,' she rambled.

Cecilia shook her head. 'Millie, it's alright. I know you don't want to go back to Cambridge. I'm not going to make you return, I promise,' she assured her.

As far as Millie knew, Cecilia wasn't someone who broke promises. She was safe. Millie let that feeling of security sink in.

'So, you'll let me stay? Isn't it a bit tricksy having your boyfriend's sister around?' Millie questioned.

In the pause before Cecilia answered, Millie felt panic set in. Evidently, it *was* awkward.

'The situation is not ideal, but it's tolerable. If you need to stay out of Cambridge, I'm more than willing to help. I want to look after you, Millie. If you don't want to stay here though, you don't have to,' Cecilia replied.

'I can't go back!' Millie cried.

When Millie saw the concern on Cecilia's face, she added: 'I want to be with family. It's Christmas.'

'Don't worry, Millie. You don't have to go back to Cambridge. What I meant was, you can be in Colchester, but not in this house. Jude's former housemate has a vacancy,' Cecilia explained.

The mention of Jude's former housemate calmed Millie. 'Oh,

Floyd? The one who practically lives on his games console? He always sounded snazzy,' she commented.

Cecilia smiled. 'Yes, he is. He still talks to Jude all the time. Floyd's just got rid of a terrible housemate, which made him really miss having Jude around. I get the feeling he's quite houseproud. That's not a problem for you though. I remember how spotless your place in Cambridge was when I visited,' she replied.

A mix of pride and longing overcame Millie. 'The *first* place I had was,' she muttered.

Before she could question what Millie meant, Cecilia heard the doorbell ring, so had to get up to answer it.

Whilst Cecilia was out of the room, Millie thought about what she'd told her. Floyd really had always sounded like a decent bloke. The idea of living with him was quite exciting. *Anything* had to be better than going back to Cambridge. She could see a problem with the plan though.

After about a minute, Cecilia returned with a plastic-wrapped parcel in her hands. She stumbled as she came into the lounge.

'Silly boy. I've told him not to leave his trainers in the way,' Cecilia muttered at the shoe she'd kicked.

To distract Cecilia from the irritation she felt towards Jude, Millie asked: 'What's that?'

Cecilia grinned. 'It's a present for Jude. Not his main one. Simply a little something for him,' she replied.

The warmth with which Cecilia said Jude's name delighted Millie. 'You really love him, don't you, even though he leaves his trainers where you can trip over them? It's very sweet,' she commented.

As her cheeks turned red, Cecilia admitted: 'Yes, I adore him.'

'That makes two of us, though I'm not in kissy-cuddly love with Jude like you are,' Millie said.

'You two seem really close. He's always there for you, you know. You could talk to him about anything,' Cecilia pointed out.

As she didn't agree with Cecilia, Millie didn't answer her. She allowed herself to be swept away by pleasant memories of how nice it had been when she and Jude had both lived in the family home.

'I'm here for you too, Millie. The love of my life adores you, and so do I. If I can help with anything, please let me know,' Cecilia added.

The kind words left Millie with a lump in her throat. If she dwelt on them, tears would follow. The last thing she wanted was to start crying during the day as well as at night.

To move on, Millie told Cecilia: 'You could help me by telling Floyd I'd love to move in.'

Cecilia nodded. 'Consider it done,' she declared.

Only then did Millie remember she'd spotted a flaw in Cecilia's plan. 'Actually, please don't do that. I can't afford to pay for it,' Millie pointed out.

'Don't worry about finances. Jude and I will pay for the pleasure of keeping you here in Colchester. Consider it a Christmas present for us all. I know how much he loves you and he doesn't get to see much of you. Your presence will bring him great joy,' Cecilia assured Millie.

'Thank you,' Millie said.

'I'll have Jude give Floyd the good news when he gets home. Right now, I've got to get back to work, as long as that's alright with you,' Cecilia told Millie.

'That's satisfactual. I've got studying to do, so I'll be fine,' Millie replied.

Having planned the short and medium-term future, Cecilia and Millie separated to go about their business, both of them spending hours on their laptops.

5

Chapter Five

Thousands of pinpricks of light twinkled in the sky. At first glance, they appeared to all be brilliant white. A few minutes observation revealed some were sort-of blue. A couple were red and moved. It was possible to concentrate on the sky, for there was very little noise to distract stargazers.

One thing that threatened to take people's focus off the stars was the bitter cold. There was no wind or rain. It was simply a static chill that seeped through coats and settled on exposed faces.

To banish the cold, Jude and Cecilia had an arm on each other's shoulders as they admired the stars above them.

'As lovely as stargazing with you is, the not sleeping thing better not become a habit. I mean, how late is it now? It's gotta be after one, cos the streetlights have turned off,' Jude commented.

'Nights like this make me most happy I'm not single. There have been many times in my life when I've laid awake for hours on end, all alone with nothing but my thoughts. I felt most lonely at night, and sad. Nowadays, when I can't sleep, I listen to you snore. That comforts me,' Cecilia told Jude.

Jude snorted. 'I do not snore!' he cried.

'Jude, I love you with all my heart, and I want to spend the rest of my life with you, but you do snore. I promise you that you snore,' Cecilia argued.

Chuckles from Jude assured Cecilia he wasn't offended. Her fiancé's laughter made her happy. To show him this, she smiled at him.

'Yeah, alright. I probably do snore. You do too, but only when you've had a few glasses of prosecco,' Jude revealed.

'Oh, charming(!)' Cecilia remarked sarcastically.

This made both members of the couple laugh. It sounded loud and harsh in the still of the night, but their merriment didn't disturb anyone.

The happy atmosphere was disturbed when Jude said: 'So, she didn't even argue when you said we'd pay for her to live with Floyd? That just ain't like Millie. She's a proud girl, like all us Austen folk. She don't just take handouts from people.'

'All she did was thank me,' Cecilia whispered.

'The poor girl seems absolutely clueless that we know something's up. That's Millie all over. She's crap at hiding stuff, always has been, but has no idea she's as easy to read as a car numberplate,' Jude commented.

'As Millie isn't good at hiding things, we'll get to the bottom of it all soon, I'm sure. The truth will come out. For now, we're looking after her,' Cecilia told Jude.

'I hope you're right. Still, at least Floyd is happy to have her. More than happy, in fact. Sounds like he's looking forward to meeting her,' Jude said.

A distant siren cut through the cold night air. It raced along a road somewhere in front of Jude and Cecilia, making swift progress in the absence of traffic in its way. The houses and high fences surrounding the garden they were standing in prevented them from spotting the emergency vehicle or its flashing blue lights.

Tiredness overcame Cecilia and she yawned.

'Maybe it's time to go back to bed,' Jude suggested.

'Yes, let's head in. I don't know how Tamsyn works through the night. Sleep may have evaded me thus far, but I am exhausted,' Cecilia agreed.

The pair crept back inside, closing and locking the door as quietly as possible. They then tiptoed through the kitchen and living room to the hooks by the front door that they silently hung their coats on. When they headed upstairs to the landing, they were greeted by heavy snoring coming from the spare room. This made them grin at each other.

'Runs in the family then,' Cecilia hissed as she opened the bedroom door to let Jude in.

The hysteria that tiredness caused made this little comment hilarious to Jude and Cecilia. They muffled their giggles as they climbed into bed together.

It wasn't long before everyone in the house was sound asleep.

6

Chapter Six

For the entire drive from his house to Floyd's, Jude assured Millie Floyd was nice. When Jude mentioned for the fourth time how polite Floyd was, Millie decided she couldn't take any more.

'Yes, I know he's nice, thanks. You've spoken about Floyd fondly for many years. I'm not nervy, I'm excited,' Millie told her brother.

'Oh, sorry. I'm preaching to the band, ain't I? Yeah, Floyd is nice. You'll get on,' Jude replied.

When Cecilia pulled up outside Floyd's, Millie breathed a sigh of relief. At last, she could see the home she only had to share with someone nice.

Before it had even been knocked on, the front door was opened by a man who was exactly as Millie had pictured him. Deep brown eyes that clearly hadn't turned square despite hours of gaming welcomed her.

To get closer to the nice man she was going to live with, Millie opened the door and stepped out of the car.

'Ah, Millie! So good to finally meet you! I'm Floyd,' the nice man cried.

After closing the door behind him, Floyd closed the distance between himself and Millie. He extended his hand, which Millie took and shook. The formality of it made her giggle.

'Hi, Floyd. Thanks for this,' Millie said.

Floyd shook his head. 'Thank me? No, no, no! *I* should be thanking *you*. My bank balance insists that I have a housemate, but it also demands I work. Finding time to search for a housemate has been impossible, so I'm lucky you came along,' he argued.

'*I'm* the lucky one. I get to be near my family in the run-up to Christmas without having to live with them,' Millie pointed out.

'I get how good that is because most of my family have moved to France. However, I get to continue to pay the rent whilst getting to know my good friend's sister, so I still think luck is on my side,' Floyd said.

As she was tired of the conversation, Millie gave up on it.

Whilst Millie and Floyd had been arguing about who was the luckiest, Jude and Cecilia had got out of the car and locked it. They were therefore ready to enter the house.

When Floyd realised Jude, Cecilia, and Millie were standing around in the cold, he reached into his pocket and produced a shiny silver key. There was a wooden keyring attached to the key that had had the name "Milly" burnt into it with a pyrography pen. Floyd handed the keyring to the person whose name was misspelt on it.

'As this is your home for a while, would you like to do the honours?' Floyd asked Millie as he handed over her key.

Though Millie took her key, she didn't tell Floyd she'd use it. This was because she was admiring the keyring on it.

As her thumb stroked over the tactile wood of her new keyring, Millie murmured: 'You had this made for me.'

Floyd shrugged. 'I just thought it was a nice welcome gift,' he commented.

'Yeah, it's lovely. Now please, Millie, could you use it to get us in? I'm freezing,' Jude complained.

As she didn't want her beloved brother to freeze, Millie opened the door. It led her to the bottom of the stairs, where there was an answerphone on the windowsill. A little green light on it flashed.

Instead of climbing the stairs, Millie turned right and went through the door to the lounge. Her eye was drawn to the television, for it was the biggest feature in the room and dominated one corner of it.

Entering the house first gave Millie a couple of seconds to appreciate the lounge by herself before Floyd, Jude, and Cecilia joined her in it.

'So, this is our lounge. I hope it's okay,' Floyd said.

'The telly is huge!' Millie gasped.

'It belongs to the landlord. He bought himself a bigger one and then asked me if he could put his old one in this property. Obviously, I said yes,' Floyd explained.

'That will be great for watching Strictly,' Millie commented.

'You love that too!' Floyd cried.

'Oh, no! That's that dancey show, ain't it? Don't tell me you like it too, Floyd,' Jude said.

Millie didn't hear her brother, for she and Floyd were singing: 'Da da da da da da dah, da da da da dah!'

'I'll go and get the bags,' Jude muttered as he walked away from his Stricty-theme-singing sister.

To help her fiancé, Cecilia followed Jude.

'I'm going to check on dinner. Why don't you help Jude take the bags up? Then you can see your room,' Floyd suggested.

'Yes, of course. See you soon,' Millie agreed.

Floyd watched Millie skip out of the room with a smile on his face. When he caught himself in the mirror, he shook his head and wandered off to the kitchen.

-

The room was smaller than the one Millie had left behind in Cambridge, but she felt much more comfortable in it. It didn't matter to her that, when you walked through the door, you were greeted by the side of a wardrobe. Experience had taught her who you shared a house with mattered much more than its interior design.

'I know it ain't much, but trust me, it's comfortable enough. I've gotta say, it's weird that you're gonna be in my old room,' Jude commented when he caught up with Millie.

'I like that it's not too frillyfied. It will be wonderful,' Millie replied.

To let Jude into the bedroom so he could put the bags down, Millie threw herself on the bed. Her head landed on the pillows.

'Ooh, these are plumpfy! I think I'm going to feel comfy here,' Millie announced.

'That's good,' Cecilia said as she too entered the room.

With three people in it, Millie's new bedroom seemed quite small. This didn't bother her though, for she never intended to have three people in it again. She didn't plan on sharing the bedroom with anyone.

'That's all your bags up here. We'll leave you to unpack. If you need us, we'll be downstairs,' Cecilia told Millie.

When Jude hesitated, Cecilia cleared her throat and looked at him in a way that told him they needed to give Millie a few minutes alone.

Left alone in her room, Millie sat up on the bed. Only then did she notice the bouquet on the bedside table. Red roses, tulips, pinecones, and foliage had been placed artfully in a simple glass vase. The arrangement filled Millie with Christmas cheer.

The bouquet, combined with the wooden keyring attached to Millie's new key, suggested Floyd cared about her. As they'd only just met, that seemed odd to her. Why go to all that effort for someone you don't know?

As she wanted to get to know Floyd better, Millie left her bags full of belongings in her room and headed downstairs.

When Millie entered the lounge, she found Cecilia crouched down scanning the spines on Floyd's sleek white melamine bookcase. There were many to read, for it was crammed full. On top of rows of paperbacks standing vertically, Floyd had slotted yet more paperbacks laying down, spines facing out so Cecilia could see their titles and how well-read some of them were.

'Floyd and Jude are in the kitchen. Apparently, dinner will be ready in ten minutes,' Cecilia told Millie.

For a moment, Millie wondered if Cecilia could read her mind. She'd answered the question Millie had been just about to ask. Deciding that was impossible, Millie joined Cecilia by the bookcase.

'So, what does Floyd read?' Millie asked.

'These are all romance novels. I can tell by the sweet titles,' Cecilia replied.

'Lovey-dovey books? That's nice,' Millie commented.

Having read all the titles, Cecilia left the books behind in favour of the L-shaped sofa. The cushion sank considerably when she sat on it. This put a frown on her face.

When Millie joined Cecilia on the sofa, she understood why her future sister-in-law looked unhappy. The tired piece of furniture was very uncomfortable.

Before Millie could work out the best way to sit on the old sofa, Floyd strolled in from the kitchen. 'I'm now ready to dish up. There's no space for a dining table, so we'll be eating off our laps. Sorry about that,' he announced.

'You're cooking for me. That's lovely. I'm not going to complain,' Millie replied.

With a smile on his face, Floyd returned to the kitchen.

-

For his guests and new housemate, Floyd had cooked sirloin steak and dauphinoise potatoes, which he served with a red wine sauce. It was delicious and impressed Millie, but she found it hard to eat on her lap. The sauce threatened to escape the plate and stain her jeans several times.

'That was very fancy,' Millie commented when she'd finished.

'I don't often have people round and I wanted to impress you. I feel I ought to mention though, that it's all from one of the German discounters,' Floyd explained.

'You don't have to buy fancy food for me, faffery in the kitchen is unnecessary, but consider me impressed,' Millie replied.

A slight redness appeared on Floyd's cheeks.

Having finished his food, Jude got up with the empty plate. Floyd jumped to his feet before Jude had taken a single step and took the plate from his hands.

After taking Cecilia's plate, Floyd said: 'You are guests in this house. I'll clear the plates and wash up.'

'Oh, that's great. Cheers! I ain't gonna argue with that,' Jude replied.

As no-one argued with him, Floyd headed off to the kitchen with everyone's plates to wash them up.

When Floyd was out of earshot, Jude told Millie in a hushed voice: 'We have to go soon. Will you be alright?'

'Of course I will. I've got a new home, and *she's* not here. I'll be fine,' Millie replied.

'Yes, Floyd seems like a great housemate. Probably better than students,' Cecilia commented.

'Oh, definitely! So much better than...' Millie agreed. She tailed off when she realised she'd almost revealed something she had to keep to herself.

'Better than?' Cecilia questioned.

'Erm, well, just better than students, as you say,' Millie told Cecilia.

Cecilia nodded. 'Living with good people is important. My brother was quite challenging to live with and so was my dad at times. I'm lucky Mum was there for my childhood, and I was able to move out after she passed away. I can't imagine how hard it is to share a home with strangers like you do,' she said.

'I never said anything was wrong at home!' Millie cried.

'No. I never said anything was wrong at your home either,' Cecilia calmly pointed out.

That was true, and Millie had no answer to that. She stayed silent and took a moment to calm down.

Into the silent room walked Floyd. 'Right, washing up is all done. Is there anything I can do for you?' he asked.

'We're fine, thank you. We'll head off home in a few minutes,' Cecilia replied.

As he knew there would soon be goodbye hugs, Floyd didn't bother to sit down. Instead he leaned on the bookcase and watched Millie play with her hair.

-

When Jude hugged Millie goodbye, he held her for several more seconds than Cecilia had, and he reminded her he was just a few minutes drive away.

Leaving Millie was more challenging than Jude had anticipated. On every step from the house to the car, he felt as if there were lead weights in his shoes. Only the knowledge he'd left his sister with a man he knew and trusted, and his fiancée's hand in his, kept him walking.

Once they were in the car, Jude asked Cecilia: 'Do you get

the impression that it's a housemate back in Cambridge upsetting Millie?'

Cecilia nodded. 'Almost certainly. A girl,' she agreed.

'Then have I done the worst thing possible by making her live with someone she don't know?' Jude questioned.

Just like she had when they'd walked out of Floyd's house together, Cecilia clutched Jude's hand. 'Don't worry, Jude. You've been a great brother. Millie will be fine with Floyd,' she assured him.

There was nothing more Cecilia could do for Jude except drive him home, which she did.

7

Chapter Seven

'So, what would you like to do for the rest of the evening?' Floyd asked Millie once they were alone together.

'Whatever you would normally do,' Millie replied.

Floyd's eyes were drawn to his bookcase. It was as if his novels were calling out to be read. It was something he considered to be antisocial though, and he wanted to be a good host for Millie.

Seeing the conflict on Floyd's face, Millie said: 'Truthfully, just tell me what you'd normally do.'

'I'd read for an hour or two. That would mean ignoring you though,' Floyd revealed.

Millie smiled. 'Floyd, you're not here to entertain me. I'll read too. It's a huge part of my studies,' she told him.

That was all the encouragement Floyd needed. He headed straight over to the bookcase and pulled out a novel with a bluey-purple cover.

Once he'd sat down with his book, Floyd declared: 'Right, I'm off to Edinburgh.'

'Good. I'll just get my book,' Millie replied.

-

A few minutes after she'd left the lounge, Millie returned with a book and two notebooks. She curled up on the opposite end of the sofa to Floyd, opened her book, and took herself off to the past.

As he was engrossed by his story, Floyd didn't acknowledge Millie's return. He didn't notice her click her pen on and off as she wrote notes. His mind was elsewhere.

About ten minutes into the romance novel, Floyd read a line that stopped him in his tracks. His eyes stopped scrolling along the page and his heart seemed to stop beating (though it didn't, thank goodness). He closed the book and placed it on the sofa next to him.

As the paragraph she was reading hadn't captured her attention, Millie noticed Floyd was staring at the wall. She put her own book down and asked: 'Are you alright?'

Floyd nodded. 'Yeah. I'm just worried for them,' he replied.

'For who?' Millie questioned.

'Star and Finn,' Floyd explained, gesturing at the book in his hand.

'But they're not real,' Millie pointed out.

'Yeah, I know. They were written to provoke real emotions though,' Floyd said.

Floyd's point gave Millie pause for thought. She picked up one of her notebooks and jotted something down in it.

'Are you taking notes?' Floyd asked.

'I am. I am noting that words of fiction evoke real feelings, especially those written to do so,' Millie explained.

'Wow, you're clever,' Floyd uttered.

'Thank you. You inspired me, so you could say you're clever too,' Millie replied with a beaming smile on her face.

Floyd snorted. 'My teachers would disagree with you, though I did pass English and maths at GCSE level,' he argued.

Instead of answering Floyd, Millie picked up her phone and started scrolling through a list on it. Her finger swiped up the screen again and again. It confused and worried Floyd that Millie was suddenly ignoring him. He couldn't work out why what he'd said would make her uncomfortable.

After almost a minute of scrolling, Millie paused. 'Science is organised knowledge. Wisdom is organised life,' she read from her screen.

'What?' Floyd questioned.

'I think it means you don't have to be academic to be clever,' Millie explained.

'What a perfect way of summing it up! You really are clever!' Floyd cried.

Millie blushed. 'Thank you, but that's not a Millie Austin original. A German philosopher said that,' she revealed.

'Well, what a clever chap he was,' Floyd commented.

'The same man said that indigenous Americans were lazy people who cared for nothing and couldn't be educated. He also claimed black people could only be educated as slaves. He didn't say black people though, but used a word I can't say,' Millie added.

'Then I take that back. He isn't clever. He's a racist arsehole!' Floyd declared.

Millie shrugged. 'He was both clever and racist. That's humans. We are a million different things all at once. What we're labelled as depends on who's labelling us, and what they know about us,' she replied.

'How profound,' Floyd said.

When Millie realised she'd been talking about philosophy to her housemate, she put her phone down and let her head fall into her hands.

'What, Millie? What's wrong?' Floyd asked.

'Oh, I've been banging on about my studies again, haven't I? I should know not to bore those unfortunate enough to live with me with the words of dead thinky people. Kayleigh has told me enough times. Sorry,' Millie apologised.

Floyd shook his head. 'Oh, Millie, you're not boring. Far from it! You're the smartest girl I've ever met, and so interesting. I could talk to you for hours,' he told her.

Millie let her gaze meet Floyd's and was struck by how soft his brown eyes were. Something about the way he was looking at her made her feel like the most special girl in the world.

'No-one's ever told me I'm interesting without meaning it sarcastically,' Millie realised out loud.

'You *are* interesting. I can't believe you've waltzed into my life,' Floyd replied.

A silence fell between Millie and Floyd that was filled by an unseen, unspoken connection between the pair. They couldn't look away from each other, but they had no idea what was bonding them.

When Floyd realised the nature of the feelings drawing him to Millie, he broke eye contact with her. 'I can see why you and Jude get on so well,' he commented

'Oh, yes! He's a wonderful brother. We've had such fun together over the years,' Millie said, grinning as she recalled all the silly things she'd done with Jude.

'He was a good housemate too. So easy to live with,' Floyd commented.

'I hope I turn out to be a good housemate,' Millie thought out loud.

Floyd swiftly replied: 'You've already shown that you are.'

-

As she snuggled into her new bed with plumpfy pillows, Millie played Floyd's words over and over in her head. He'd been so nice to her. That niceness had seeped into her very soul. She was too happy to notice she cried no tears before falling asleep that night.

8

Chapter Eight

A plate of toast was waiting for Millie on the kitchen worktop when she got downstairs on her first morning in Floyd's house. The buttery scent drew her to it.

'Good morning, Millie! I took the liberty of making you some toast,' Floyd told her.

'Ooh, scumptulicious! Please feel free to do that every morning. Thank you,' Millie cried.

Without further ado, Millie grabbed the plate and took it back to the lounge where she sat on the sofa and scoffed the toast.

Whilst Millie ate her toast, Floyd told her: 'I've got the day off work today. I was thinking we could pop into town and do some shopping. I've got food, I just want household bits, and hair clippers, because mine finally gave up on me at the weekend.'

As she had a mouthful of food, so couldn't speak, Millie nodded her approval.

'Do you have a good coat? It's a bit of a walk,' Floyd asked.

'I walk everywhere in Cambridge, I can't drive or cycle, so I have a coat that keeps me toasty,' Millie replied.

'You can't drive? Neither can I. That's why we're walking,' Floyd explained.

Millie nodded. 'My parents couldn't afford to pay for lessons *and* give me spending money for uni. When offered the choice between being free from the demands of a part-time job whilst studying or learning to drive, I chose the former,' she revealed.

'It is so expensive. That's what put me off,' Floyd commented.

'Many useful skills, like driving, are inaccessible to a lot of people just because of money,' Millie said.

That was all Millie had to say about money and driving lessons, so she continued eating her toast.

It was evident Millie loved her toast, for it didn't stay on her plate for long. This was one of many things that made Floyd feel they really were quite similar.

-

It came as a pleasant surprise to Floyd to discover the weather outside his front door was cold, but mild. When Millie joined him, he noticed her big, fur-lined boots.

'They're clompy, but keep my tootsies nice and warm,' Millie explained when she saw where Floyd was looking.

'Very nice,' Floyd commented.

'Thanks. The boots were a birthday prezzie from Maddie,' Millie revealed.

As he didn't know who Maddie was, Floyd didn't say anything about that. He just locked his front door and headed off into the city with Millie.

Not long after stepping out of the front door, Millie found herself in a park. A wide and solid path swept round bare trees devoid of leaves. It was a place that felt completely different in winter than it did in summer. She could see why the Christmas carol described midwinter as bleak.

Unlike the weather, Millie wasn't bleak. She was as chirpy as the birds absent from Castle Park on that day. 'It's great to shop with someone. It makes buying even boring things much more fun,' she declared.

'Yes, company is good,' Floyd agreed.

'Maddie and I always do the weekly shop together. That's partly because the other housemates are too lazy to do it, one of them I hardly ever see, but also just because we'll take any excuse to be together,' Millie told Floyd.

The mention of Maddie's name again caught Floyd's attention. She was clearly important.

'You two have a very sweet relationship,' Floyd commented.

'Oh, we do. My life wasn't complete until I met Maddie. I've really settled since we met, and I've been so happy. Two peas in a pod, we are. People refer to us as M and M,' Millie enthused.

This reminded Floyd of how he used to feel about Millie's brother. They hadn't had a cute joint nickname like M&M, but they'd done almost everything together.

As she walked, Millie wondered why Floyd was suddenly subdued and quiet. She then realised they were on a sustained uphill. It may be that he was focusing on the effort of fighting the cold and the incline.

When Millie and Floyd reached the castle at the top of the hill, the peace of the park was replaced by the noise of the city centre. Busses rumbled down the street, people shouted as they greeted one another, and a bell in a clock tower rose above the din to announce the time.

The cacophony continued as Millie and Floyd made their way across the High Street and along the side roads. This prevented them from chatting.

The chain chemist Floyd led Millie to gave them respite from the hustle and bustle of the city. That allowed Millie to say: 'I'm glad we've come here. I need to get something for myself.'

Floyd nodded and replied: 'Go ahead.'

After glancing up at the signs, Millie made her way to the period products aisle. Floyd followed without giving it much thought. Once she'd located the correct shelf, she removed a few packets of night-time sanitary towels.

It took Floyd a few seconds to realise what Millie was buying. When he did, he blushed. Millie saw this and laughed, which only made him blush harder.

'It's a perfectly natural process. Most people who menstruate have to buy products like these every month,' Millie pointed out.

When Millie said this, Floyd recalled hearing a similar voice talk about periods once. It wasn't a subject he discussed often, so he wasn't sure who he was thinking of or where he'd heard a voice like Millie's before.

'Erm, yes. I was just surprised. I was surprised that you picked up sanitary towels. I mean, I thought you'd use tampons,' Floyd stammered.

'I'm scared of Toxic Shock Syndrome,' Millie explained.

'Erm, is that something that comes from tampons then?' Floyd asked.

'No, it's a bacteria thing. Tampons don't cause it, and they are safe really. There are various ways to get it, and it's quite rare, like struck by lightning rare. It's just that I've read too many horror stories. The risk of TSS is slightly less with pads, so that's what I use. It makes me more comfortable,' Millie explained.

'Okay,' Floyd replied.

The way Floyd was squirming and couldn't quite look at her made Millie smile. 'Like I said, periods are natural. If you live with someone who menstruates, you should know their cycle. Trust me, you'll thank me for that advice one day when your housemate is full of nastiness and then you look at the calendar and realise it's about hormones, not you. I know. I've lived with menstruating people for years,' she told Floyd.

'Yeah, cheers. Cheers for that advice,' Floyd muttered.

It didn't surprise Millie at all when, a few seconds later, Floyd said: 'I'm just going to go and do some shopping for myself. Meet me by Holy Trinity Church, please.'

Never had Millie seen someone walk as quickly through a shop as Floyd did to get away from the period products aisle. After laughing to herself once again, Millie made her way to the checkout.

-

When Millie got to Holy Trinity Church, having queued for ages in the chemist, Floyd was already waiting. He was leaning on the black railings and watching a smartly-dressed man and a pink-haired woman in front of him. The man in a suit was holding hands with the woman with colourful hair. It seemed that he was sharing something important with her. Then, just as Millie reached Floyd, the smart man got down on one knee and produced a little box from the inside pocket of his suit jacket. The pink-haired woman's hands flew up to her face as she gasped in shock. Now Millie knew what she was watching.

'Dearest Eugenie, light of my life, will you make me the happiest man on Earth and do me the honour of becoming my wife?' the man on one knee asked the pink-haired woman.

By now, tears were flooding out of Eugenie's eyes. 'Oh, yes! Yes, yes, yes!' she cried.

It wasn't just Eugenie who was crying. Floyd was crying too. He, Millie, and a couple of other random passers-by applauded as the man in a suit slid a diamond ring onto Eugenie's finger. As soon as the smart man was back on his feet, Eugenie kissed him.

'I love you, Hamish,' Eugenie told her now-fiancé.

Hamish chuckled. 'I should hope so. We're going to get married,' he pointed out.

In response, Eugenie kissed Hamish three times, letting her lips linger on his for quite a few seconds on her third attempt. 'Love you, love you, love you,' she repeated.

To calm Eugenie, Hamish laid a gentle kiss on her forehead and whispered in her ear. The happy couple then linked arms and headed off down the lane, giggling as they went.

The grin on Floyd's face was almost as big as the one on Hamish's. 'That's one of the best things I've ever seen,' he said.

'It was very sweet. I love the idea of getting engaged outside a beautiful building like this church. You'd feel that history was on your side,' Millie commented.

Though it wasn't at all related to what she was talking about, Millie's eye was drawn to the carrier bag in Floyd's hand.

'I've got everything for me now, and a little something for you,' Floyd told Millie.

Before Millie could ask what he'd bought for her, Floyd removed the chocolate bar from the bag and handed it over.

'I've heard that some girls like flowers and chocolate on their period. I didn't have time for flowers, but chocolate was easy to get. I hope you like this one. It's light and bubbly, like you,' Floyd explained.

As she tore open her Aero bar, Millie said: 'I am one of those girls. I'm not on until the end of the week, but thanks for this. I'll have it immediately, in preparation for mensuration.'

Whilst Millie enjoyed the sweetness of the chocolate bar Floyd had bought her, she wandered home through Castle Park with him.

9

Chapter Nine

'Wow, I loved that Foxtrot,' Millie said as the end titles of Strictly Come Dancing rolled.

'Yeah, me too. So skilful,' Floyd agreed.

'The freckles were really good,' Millie added.

Though Floyd knew the move Millie was referring to was a fleckerl, not a freckle, he didn't correct her. The mistake amused him.

A buzz from her phone made Millie pick it up. After smiling at the message on screen, Millie held the phone out in front of her and took a selfie of her doing a thumbs up.

'Maddie and I use expressive selfies instead of emojis. We watch Strictly together every week, and I was just letting her know what I thought. She's just saying that the couple's choice made her cry,' Millie revealed.

'You two really are close,' Floyd commented.

'We're the best of friends. I'm really looking forward to seeing her next week. She's invited me to her birthday party back in Cambridge,' Millie said.

'Oh, so you're going away?' Floyd asked.

Millie nodded. 'Only for one night though,' she told Floyd.

Early next week, Floyd was going on a date. He wondered if it would be on the night Millie was away.

'It's always hard to know what to do after Strictly,' Millie commented.

'I usually play video games. Most of the weekend is dedicated to gaming,' Floyd revealed.

'Great! I've never really played video games. That'll be fun,' Millie declared.

Though he hadn't intended to play video games with Millie, Floyd agreed it would be fun. He got up to turn one of his consoles on and get the remotes.

-

After firing a red shell at the kart in front of hers, Millie found herself in second place with one lap to go. Quick reactions allowed her to dodge a banana skin that had been dumped on the track. She was totally focused.

Ahead of Millie was Floyd, with a half a lap lead. He noticed that, if he continued at his current speed, he'd beat her. Once he was sure of this, Floyd pulled a hard right turn and drove his kart straight into the river.

All Millie was aware of was her part of the screen. Her hands moved fluidly to keep her kart on the track. After some twisty bends, she spotted another kart ahead of her. It was too far in front for her to catch. She was doomed to second place. Despite the disappointment of this, Millie continued to drive as hard as she could. The kart in front wasn't driving so well. It seemed to find every obstacle on the course. This allowed Millie to race past and take pole position, which she kept all the way to the finish line.

'Yay, I won!' Millie cried.

Floyd smiled at his housemate. 'Yes, you did. Well done,' he said.

'Can we play more? Please?' Millie begged.

'Of course,' Floyd agreed.

Once Floyd had chosen a track, Millie zoned in on the TV screen. She was quick off the mark and kept up with the computer-controlled leaders of the race. Along with the leaders, she followed a sweeping bend round a large fountain. This led to a narrow alley.

Whilst his kart on screen curved round the fountain, Floyd watched Millie in real life. She moved her body on the sharp turns, as if shifting her weight in the real world would help her kart navigate the virtual track. Her eyes were focused on the TV screen and full of determination. The only other person Floyd had played this game with was Millie's brother, who raced carelessly and didn't bother to concentrate. The difference between the siblings was stark.

A speed boost put Millie ahead of her rivals before the end of the first lap. Her lead over second place was dramatically reduced when she hit a banana skin and her kart span out. She growled in frustration but managed to just about stay in first.

Floyd advanced through the ranks and managed to get in sight of Millie and the second placed kart. This meant he saw the moment when the computer-controlled player threw a shell at Millie's kart, which allowed them to get past.

'Silly-Toady!' Millie snapped.

'I've shouted at the computer whilst playing this many times,' Floyd told Millie.

'Shush! I'm driving,' Millie replied.

After smashing through an item box, Millie acquired a red shell, which she immediately threw. It found the character in front and flipped their kart. This tit-for-tat revenge got Millie back into the lead.

The shell Millie threw helped Floyd get right behind the computer player she'd demoted to second place. An item box gave him a speed boost that would be enough to get him past the computer and possibly Millie as well to claim first place. After aiming at the computer-controlled character that had troubled Millie so much, Floyd released his speed boost. The troublesome rival was shoved off the track into the sea. Floyd himself lost control and careered into a wall. This gave Millie a comfortable lead.

Oblivious to the drama behind her, Millie was enjoying having the track to herself. She soared over the bridge, round the corner, and across the finish line. Starting the final lap in first place filled her with confidence.

As her final lap was faultless, no-one was able to pass Millie. She won her second race.

'Congratulations,' Floyd said when Millie crossed the line well ahead of him.

'This is great, not just because I'm winning!' Millie cried.

Thanks to accidentally hitting a wall right near the end of the race, Floyd placed third. It didn't affect his enjoyment at all.

'I've enjoyed this since I was a teenager. It's fun,' Floyd told Millie.

'I get so caught up in the game that I forget all about real life. I've never known anything that's such a good stress reliever. Well, only one thing, which I don't do anymore,' Millie declared.

Though he wondered what Millie thought was a better stress reliever than gaming, Floyd didn't ask. It was obvious to him she wanted to keep whatever it was to herself, and he respected her privacy. He was most curious about why she'd stopped doing this thing she enjoyed.

'Well, if ever you get stressed, let me know. I'm never going to say no to Mario Kart,' Floyd said.

'Thank you, but she'd mock that too, which would just make me more stressed,' Millie replied.

'She? Who is she? Who would mock you for gaming?' Floyd questioned.

Millie's eyes widened. 'Oh, erm, no-one. I meant that I'd be worried about getting behind on my studies,' she lied.

Floyd nodded slowly. 'Right. I see. Just so you know, "no-one" has no right to mock anything you do, including play video games,' he told Millie.

As she'd denied the person Floyd was referring to existed, Millie didn't know how to answer. "No-one" wasn't someone she felt she could talk about.

'If you'd like to talk about this clearly horrible woman, I'm here for you. If not, let's race again,' Floyd said.

'That shopping centre course looks fun,' Millie replied.

'I understand,' Floyd told Millie as he selected the track she was referring to.

Within a few seconds, Millie was once again lost in the pixellated world of karts driven by colourful characters.

10

Chapter Ten

The second Millie got through the door of her student house, she was wrapped up in Maddie's arms.

'Hello, gorgeous girl! I'm so happy we're back together,' Maddie said.

'Me too. Happy birthday,' Millie replied.

When Maddie realised Millie was still holding her suitcase, she released her friend. This allowed her to kiss Millie on both cheeks.

'Do you mind if I put this in my room?' Millie asked.

'Not at all. I'll have a cup of tea waiting for you in the kitchen. I got some Assam teabags for a treat,' Maddie told Millie.

Excitement made Millie rush up the stairs. After bursting into her room, she paused. It was bigger than her room at Floyd's. The furniture was much more modern. The room she slept in in Colchester felt more comfortable than the one she was standing in now, despite the size difference.

'Well, well, Emily. You know you don't have to eat *all* the trimmings at Christmas dinner, don't you?' a voice behind Millie said.

As she'd not heard Kayleigh, the source of the voice, approach, Millie jumped.

'There's no need to leap about, silly girl,' Kayleigh told Millie.

Anger made Millie dump her bag on the floor and spin round to face her housemate. 'Kayleigh,' she said.

'Ugh, my name sounds atrocious in your stupid common accent,' Kayleigh commented.

'I'm not stupid at all. I'm a very clever girl,' Millie replied.

Kayleigh smirked. 'You just keep telling yourself that, Emily. Anyway, I've got better things to do than talk to you. Laters,' she said.

Much to Millie's relief, Kayleigh walked off.

'And that's why I've been dreading coming back,' Millie muttered to herself.

To keep herself safe from Kayleigh for a few minutes, Millie stepped inside her room and slammed the door. She felt her face get hotter and hotter. Tears prickled behind her eyes.

When she got notified of a text, Millie whipped her phone out. It was just the distraction she needed. The text was from Floyd, asking if she'd got to Cambridge safely. As she had got to Cambridge safely, Millie told him so.

The caring text from Floyd shoved the hurt Kayleigh had put there out of Millie's heart and replaced it with warmth. That was boosted when Millie remembered how pleased Maddie had been to see her. The feelings told her all she needed was to be with nice people.

Before she could be with Maddie, Millie wanted to change. It was a party, after all, and she'd travelled up in jeans and a t-shirt. Maddie herself was wearing jeans, and wouldn't care if Millie continued to do so, but Millie fancied wearing a dress. It would make it feel more like a special occasion to her, and Maddie's birthday definitely was that.

-

A few minutes after opening her wardrobe, Millie descended the stairs carrying a tall, thin gift bag and wearing a floaty navy-blue flowery dress. When she got down to the kitchen-diner, she found Maddie waiting for her next to a mug of black tea. The mug was handed to Millie as soon as Maddie saw her.

A sip of the dark, malty tea filled Millie with energy. 'Wow! This tea has that make-you-shiver goosebumpablility. Thanks for buying it,' she said.

Maddie smiled. 'Anything for you. Loving the dress by the way. You look beautiful,' she told Millie.

To best show off her dress, Millie twirled, just about keeping her tea in her mug as she did so. 'It's swishy. I love it too. You look beautifuler,' she replied.

After realising what she'd said, Millie added: 'Well, not *fuller*.'

Maddie noticed the bag in Millie's left hand. 'Is that for me?' she asked her.

Millie nodded enthusiastically. 'Yes, your prezzie. I hope you like it,' she confirmed.

To check if she liked it, Maddie took the bag from Millie. Then, far slower than Millie would have liked, she removed the bottle of strawberry laces gin from it. The grin on Maddie's face told Millie what she thought of the gift.

'That may not last long. Thank you, gorgeous girl,' Maddie told Millie.

Once Maddie had put her gift safely on the kitchen side and Millie had dumped her mug of tea next to it, the pair hugged. It was a long, warm embrace, ending only when the doorbell rang.

'Ah, that'll be the hot guys I ordered,' Maddie announced.

'What? Surely you didn't get strippers,' Millie questioned.

Maddie laughed. 'Unfortunately not. They're just a few good-looking people who also study Human, Social, and Political Sciences. They will be keeping their clothes on this evening,' she explained.

When the doorbell rang again, Maddie left Millie to go and answer it.

As Maddie had said, the new arrivals were guys who were hot. The tallest of the four men caught Millie eye. She couldn't help smiling at him. In response, he winked, which made her blush.

It wasn't just the hot guys who entered the room. Kayleigh, who had been absent, also made an appearance. She walked straight up to one of the men and engaged him in conversation. Thankfully, he wasn't one Millie wanted.

The man who Millie *did* want began to approach her, step by agonisingly slow step. It felt like it took him an hour to cross the room when in fact it was just a few seconds. Her heart beat faster and faster as he got closer.

When he reached her, the man extended his hand to Millie. 'Daniel,' he told her.

Millie gave Daniel her hand and was amused by how small it seemed in his. 'I'm Millie,' she replied.

A slow smile spread across Daniel's face. 'The other half of M and M. At last, I can put a face to the name, and a pretty one at that. Maddie is always talking about you,' he said.

Being called pretty made Millie giggle. 'Erm, thanks,' she whispered.

'I think I'm going to enjoy this evening,' Daniel commented.

'Oh, me too!' Millie eagerly agreed.

After looking over his shoulder, Daniel told Millie: 'I need to save Bradley from that blonde. He's giving off all his "help me" signs. Don't worry though. I'll be back.'

As she watched Daniel walk away to separate his friend from Kayleigh, Millie held onto the counter for support. She had a feeling the night was going to be a good night.

11

Chapter Eleven

Bright, shining lights adorned some of the houses that Floyd walked past on his way into town.

The restaurant that was Floyd's destination had a big Christmas tree just inside the door. It towered over him and the sign telling him to wait to be seated. He watched the lights twinkle whilst doing as the sign instructed.

'Floyd?' a voice behind him said.

As he suspected he would, Floyd turned round to find his date standing there. 'Dani, hi! A pleasure to meet you,' he told her.

The pair awkwardly shook hands.

'You're early,' Floyd pointed out.

'Yeah, well, my shoot didn't take as long as they said it would. Thought I may as well get down here early, didn't I?' Dani replied.

'Erm, yes, you did,' Floyd agreed.

At this point, the waiter turned up to show Floyd and Dani to their table. He failed to offer to take Floyd's coat. Dani didn't have a coat to take. All she was wearing was her little black dress.

When they reached the table, Floyd got a little bit ahead and pulled Dani's chair out for her.

'Oh, stop it! That is so cute!' Dani cried as she sat down on the chair.

'I'm just being a gentleman,' Floyd told Dani as he pushed her chair in.

Once Dani was seated to his satisfaction, Floyd himself took a seat.

'So, you mentioned a shoot. Was that a photoshoot? I remember your profile saying you're a model,' Floyd asked.

'Yeah. My dream is to be a film star, or at least do decent telly ads. I'm just a model for now though. Do ads for catalogues, skincare range, a lingerie brand once, stuff like that. It gets me money, you know?' Dani revealed.

Whilst nodding, Floyd went to take a sip of his drink. He then realised he didn't have a drink yet.

'What will you have to drink?' Floyd asked Dani and himself.

'Porn star martini. It's just a bit of me in a drink,' Dani answered immediately.

A second later Dani gasped and her hands flew up to her mouth. 'Oh my days, that came out wrong! When I were talking about wanting to be a film star, that ain't the kind of film I meant! I just like passion fruit!' she squealed.

For the first time since she'd walked through the door, Floyd felt a little spark of attraction for Dani. He laughed with her about the humorous mistake.

~

True to her word, Dani ordered a porn star martini when the waiter came over. Both she and Floyd grinned when she had to say it out loud. As his date was having a cocktail, Floyd felt he should as well. He chose the same. Food was ordered at the waiter's request, so he wouldn't have to return for a while.

'What do you look for in a man?' Floyd asked.

'Short hair, taller than me, good dress sense, looks after me, looks after themselves, that sort of thing. I don't like them boys that mess you about, you know? I'm not here to play games,' Dani revealed.

Inside, Floyd did a happy dance. He considered himself to be exactly what Dani was looking for.

'Exactly! The Nintendo Wii is for playing games with, not girls,' Floyd agreed.

Dani laughed. 'The Wii? That's well old news. I had it as a kid, but got bored of it. It weren't a proper console,' she commented.

This didn't seem like the right time to Floyd to mention he owned a Wii which he used regularly and loved. A memory of Millie sprang to mind, leaning round corners that only existed on screen. It brought a smile to his lips.

'How do you kill time?' Dani asked.

Remembering what Dani had said about the Nintendo Wii, Floyd decided to keep one of his hobbies to himself. 'I read a lot. This is a great time of the year for that. Christmas romance novels are the best!' he enthused.

A frown creased Dani's heavily tanned and otherwise immaculate face. '*You* read romance novels?' she questioned.

'Yes. That's my favourite genre,' Floyd confirmed.

'Shut up!' Dani cried.

Floyd shrugged. 'It's true. I love reading about love,' he said.

'Oh, shut up!' Dani repeated.

This time, Floyd did as he was told.

When the drinks arrived, Floyd was very grateful. He had no idea how to move on from someone repeatedly shouting "shut up" at him because he read romance novels.

12

Chapter Twelve

After putting loud music on in the house, Maddie then took Millie to the tiny courtyard out the back so they could chat. Already there was Bradley, smoking a cigarette, and Ross, the housemate she hardly saw.

'I have to show you these pictures from Patrick's wedding!' Maddie cried.

'I saw some on Insta,' Millie told her friend.

'The nice ones were posted on there, but he refused to share my favourite,' Maddie explained.

As she scrolled through her phone, Maddie said: 'My little cousin was walking up the aisle with the rings when he tripped on the step and threw the cushion and very expensive gold rings straight at the vicar.'

After describing the scene, Maddie showed Millie a photo of it. The cushion was in mid-air, there was a horrified look on everyone's faces, and it was indeed hilarious. Millie giggled at the daft image.

'The vicar used to be a semi-professional goalie, so she caught them with ease. It did make me chuckle,' Maddie told her friend.

'I wish I could have been there,' Millie said.

'That's what Kayleigh said,' Maddie revealed.

The mention of Kayleigh dampened Millie's spirits. 'Really?' she questioned.

'I know! It's ridiculous. Yes, she's grown up next door to us, but my uncle isn't obliged to invite our neighbours. Kayleigh is not a family friend,' Maddie agreed.

It pleased Millie to hear Maddie say Kayleigh wasn't a friend. As Kayleigh had known Maddie much longer than she'd known her, Millie had never quite been sure about the nature of their relationship.

A plinky piano intro drifted out from the house that made both Millie and Maddie gasp. 'It's our song!' they squealed together.

Without another word to each other, Millie and Maddie held hands and dashed inside. They were in the middle of the main room, which had been cleared to make a dancefloor, before Idina Menzel had started singing.

Side by side, Millie and Maddie swayed to one of their favourite songs. When the chorus came, they belted it out together. This turned most of the heads in the room, but they didn't care. After all, Maddie was the birthday girl.

'This isn't a Christmas song,' someone pointed out to Maddie when she wasn't screaming out the title of the song that wasn't a Christmas song.

'The film is called *Frozen* and was released in November slash December, so I think it counts,' Maddie replied.

The someone didn't bother the birthday girl again.

When *Let It Go* ended, Millie and Maddie hugged each other.

'Happy birthday, Maddie,' Millie said.

'Oh, it *is* a happy birthday,' Maddie agreed.

The next song was just as familiar to Millie as the previous one had been. It made her smile.

'I'll be the drunk-sounding Irish guy,' Maddie told Millie.

For the next few minutes, Millie and Maddie insulted each other through song lyrics and had a whale of a time doing it. *Fairytale of New York* was a fun song to sing and dance to.

Whilst Millie was giggling about what she and Maddie had just done, Daniel approached her and extended his hand. 'May I have this dance?' he asked.

As she had been dancing with Maddie, Millie considered this quite rude. She was just about to say so when Maddie told Daniel: 'She's yours. Have fun!'

Just before she left her, Maddie winked at Millie and flashed her a cheesy grin.

Unlike Maddie, Daniel held Millie close. She could feel his hard muscles through his shirt and quite liked that. The way he towered over her also pleased her.

'Told you I'd be back,' Daniel said.

There was something husky about Daniel's voice that made it hard for Millie to speak. 'You did,' she uttered.

'Would I be right in assuming you're pleased that I'm back?' Daniel asked.

'Yeah,' Millie whispered.

'Me too,' Daniel told her.

This was all Daniel felt the need to say for a while. He simply swayed with Millie tight against him.

The warmth of Daniel and the spicy scent of his aftershave washed over Millie. She was completely relaxed in his arms.

After they'd swayed together through quite a few songs, Daniel asked: 'Can I get you a drink?'

'We can get drinks together,' Millie replied.

Daniel nodded. 'Yeah, that's cool,' he agreed.

Being released from Daniel's embrace reintroduced Millie to the world around her. She'd forgotten that it was Maddie's party. She'd forgotten that she was surrounded mostly by strangers. She'd forgotten that Kayleigh was in the same room, watching and smirking.

Ignoring everyone else, but now aware of them, Millie made her way with Daniel to the back of the room. She took the kettle out of the cupboard Maddie had hidden it away in, filled it with water, plugged it in, and clicked it on to boil.

Daniel frowned. 'What are you making?' he asked.

'A cup of tea. It's Assam, a special dark, malty, strong tea that I love,' Millie explained as she dropped a teabag into a mug.

'What? You're having tea at a party?' Daniel questioned.

'Yes,' Millie confirmed.

'Are you going to put some kind of alcohol in?' Daniel asked.

'No. Just tea,' Millie said.

Daniel shook his head. 'That's boring,' he told Millie.

The kettle had just finished boiling. Millie was tempted to pour it over Daniel instead of her teabag. Any attraction she had felt for him vanished.

'I don't drink. That doesn't make me boring,' Millie pointed out.

'If you say so,' Daniel replied.

When Daniel proceeded to walk away from her, Millie really didn't care.

What Millie *did* care about was her mug of tea. It was too hot to drink, as she hadn't added milk to it, but she was able to sniff it, admire the dark colour of the liquid in the mug, and dream about how good it would taste.

For a few seconds, Millie wondered if she was boring. When she recalled the fun she'd had with Maddie singing and dancing, and with Floyd racing pixellated karts, she concluded she wasn't.

'What happened with Daniel? I thought you two were getting on well?' Maddie asked, sidling up to Millie.

'We were. He was lovely and limby, which you know I like, and he had that goosebumpablility. Sadly, he was also judgy. He called me boring because I'm drinking tea,' Millie explained.

Maddie gasped. 'Oh, Millie! What an arse he is! You aren't boring. You're a riot,' she told her.

'Thank you. It's a shame, for him I mean, but it takes more than a pretty face and long limbs to charm me these days. I want to be *loved*,' Millie said.

With her arm around her, Maddie assured Millie: 'You deserve love, and someone out there will give it to you.'

13

Chapter Thirteen

'So, what's the damage?' Dani asked Floyd when she came back from the ladies.

Before answering Dani, or letting her get to the table, Floyd stood and pulled her chair back. Just like when they'd arrived, she sat on it and he pushed her in.

Eventually, Floyd told Dani: 'That's none of your concern. I settled the bill whilst you were away from the table.'

'Oh, that is so cute! You're a keeper,' Dani cried, fluttering her false eyelashes.

Though he'd never thought of the way he treated women as "cute", Floyd's intention was to make his dates want to stay with him, so he was pleased he'd been successful. He gave himself a mental pat on the back.

As there was still some liquid in it, Dani raised her glass and drained it. Floyd had already finished his third cocktail.

'Right, shall we make a move?' Floyd suggested.

'Sounds like a plan,' Dani agreed.

The pair left the restaurant, waving goodbye to the waiters. Once out in the cold, they both lost motion and loitered by the doors.

'Would you like me to walk you home?' Floyd offered.

'It'd be a bit of a walk. I've come from near Clacton,' Dani replied.

It would take around five hours to walk from where they were standing to Clacton. Floyd agreed that was a long walk, and so didn't offer to undertake it.

'A lift would be nice though,' Dani said.

'I don't have a car and, even if I did, I'm well over the limit,' Floyd pointed out.

Dani's eyes widened. 'Shut up! You don't have a car?' she questioned.

'I can't afford it, and I don't really need one,' Floyd told Dani.

'No way! Who doesn't have a car?!' Dani asked incredulously.

'Erm, me,' Floyd reminded his date.

'Oh, shut up!' Dani cried.

Just like the last time he'd been told to, Floyd did indeed shut up.

Several seconds passed in silence with Dani just standing there staring at Floyd. In that time, he wondered two things. The first was how Dani could cope without a coat. His second wondering was how to tell her he didn't want to see her again.

'So, you don't have a car? Nah, this ain't gonna work between us. A man's gotta have a hot set of wheels, do you know what I mean? I can't be the driver in a relationship. You've seen how much I like my porn star martinis,' Dani announced.

'Oh, that's a shame. Still, it was nice to meet you,' Floyd lied.

'Yeah, and you. Never met a guy like you. It was a cute night,' Dani replied.

What Dani said made Floyd wonder a third thing; how could a night be "cute"?

When Dani got her phone out, Floyd asked: 'How will you get home?'

'Oh, I'll get myself a cab. That's what I'm about to do,' Dani said.

'I'll wait with you, to keep you safe. I may as well have the cab swing by mine, so I don't have to walk,' Floyd told Dani.

'If you like,' Dani agreed.

Floyd did like that plan. Though he never wanted to see Dani again, he needed to know she was safety on her way home.

~

On the taxi ride to his house, there wasn't any conversation between Floyd and Dani. He could see she'd given up trying with him. Before leaving her and the cab, Floyd handed Dani a note worth far more than his share of the fare. She thanked him, said goodbye, and made no mention of swapping numbers or seeing him again.

Whilst waiting for the taxi, Floyd had gotten a little chilly. The short ride in it hadn't been enough to warm him up, so he was looking forward to getting indoors.

Once he'd got through the door, Floyd headed straight for the lounge, which wasn't as warm as he'd hoped. He noticed a big grey hoodie on the sofa, which he picked up and pulled on over his shirt. Only after he'd done this did Floyd realise the hoodie wasn't his. Millie had abandoned it there a day ago. As he hugged the comfy item of clothing round himself, he wondered how its owner was and why he missed her so much.

14

Chapter Fourteen

Having spent the morning wandering around town with Maddie, Millie felt full of love for her friend and the city they studied in. The pain of leaving Cambridge was eased slightly by the knowledge Maddie was standing on Carter Bridge, which went over the tracks just to the north of the station, ready to wave frantically when Millie's train went under. The girls wouldn't be able to see each other, but the idea was nice.

As the train passed under Carter Bridge, Millie waved at the ceiling. 'Goodbye, Maddie,' she said.

A passenger noticed this behaviour and frowned.

'My friend is on the bridge waving goodbye to me,' Millie told the frowning man, who hadn't asked for an explanation.

The passenger shook his head and went back to reading his copy of *The Daily Mail*.

As she didn't have a newspaper, Millie gazed out of the window. It wasn't long before the train escaped the city and she could see wide open fields.

-

After changing train at Ipswich, Millie began to look forward to getting back to Colchester. She found herself thinking of the little mid-terrace she shared with Floyd as home.

When the train pulled in at Colchester, Millie was waiting by the doors. She jumped out as soon as she could and was pleasantly surprised by how warm it was outside. In Cambridge it had been quite cold.

By the time Millie got home, she was a little sweaty. Her heavy coat was too much in that mild weather.

'I'm home!' Millie called as she entered the house.

In the lounge, Millie found Floyd wearing her hoodie. 'It suits you,' she told him.

As he'd forgotten he was still wearing Millie's jumper, Floyd gasped. 'Oh, sorry. I'll take it off now,' he said.

'There's no need. I'll have one of yours. Walking home in my big winter coat has left me snuggly and toasty, so I'll be alright for a while,' Millie assured Floyd.

'You won't be hot for long. The boiler is on the blink. Something must have happened while I was out last night, and now I can't get it to work,' Floyd revealed.

'Oh, that's unfortunate. Once I've stolen your jumper, we'll have to snuggle up under a blanket together to keep warm,' Millie said.

Floyd didn't answer that, and Millie left the room to remove her coat, take her suitcase upstairs, and get the jumper she knew Floyd left hanging over the banister.

In the suitcase already in Millie's room was a big crocheted blanket. She dumped her other suitcase under her bed and dug out the blanket. After cuddling it to herself, she carried it downstairs.

When he heard Millie's footsteps returning to the lounge, Floyd asked: 'How was your trip?'

'Wonderful! Maddie and I belted out *Let It Go* together like no-one was listening. Hopefully, it was everything she wanted. She's a great friend,' Millie replied.

Once she'd answered him, Millie sat down right next to Floyd on a sofa that seated five, so close that their bodies were touching, and then threw the blanket around them.

'There you go. All snuggly and toasty now,' Millie declared.

'Erm, thanks,' Floyd said, unsure what to say about Millie's proximity to him.

'Thank Nanny Millicent, who I'm sort-of named after. She crocheted this for me when she found out Mum and Dad were having a girl,' Millie told Floyd.

'That's, well, great. That's great. Aren't you called Emily though, not Millicent?' Floyd questioned.

As if thinking about her own name, Millie put a hand on her chin. Her other arm absentmindedly went round Floyd's shoulder. 'Yes, I'm Emily, but I'm usually called Millie. Nanny Millicent was also usually called Millie. As a tribute to her, I spell Millie the way she did, not M, I, L, L, Y, as most people called *Emily* would,' Millie explained.

'Oh, cool,' Floyd commented.

The conversation he'd just had made Floyd realise he'd made a mistake, which he dwelt on for a while.

When Millie tightened her arm around him, Floyd was once again aware of how close she was. He squirmed a little, but she didn't seem to notice.

'Shall I put some dinner on for us? You could choose a film while I do it. I fancy a movie night,' Floyd suggested.

'Oh, goodie! That sounds perfect!' Millie agreed.

Making tea and choosing a DVD meant Millie and Floyd had to separate. When he was in the kitchen, Floyd realised, just as she'd said, Millie and Nanny Millicent's blanket had kept him snuggly and toasty. He was getting colder by the second.

Back in the lounge, Millie had put *Frozen* in the DVD player. Just as she was about to message Maddie to let her know what she was watching, a phone call came through. Millie answered it after seeing it was from the very woman she was going to message.

'Hey, gorgeous girl! Just a quick call to let you know I'm safety back home,' Maddie explained.

There was barking in the background of the call. Maddie laughed and added: 'Trixie seems happy to have me back.'

'Oh, good. Glad you're back with the family. I'm about to watch *Frozen* with my housemate,' Millie told Maddie.

'How funny! Is this the heart-meltingly sweet housemate you were telling me about earlier?' Maddie asked.

Millie had forgotten she'd described Floyd like that only a few hours ago whilst walking to Cambridge station. 'Yes, it is the heart-meltingly sweet housemate. As you might expect of someone like that, he has almost every Disney film on DVD. I'm in heaven,' she confirmed.

A soft chuckle came down the phone. 'Dad will be back with takeaway soon, so I'll leave you to enjoy watching Disney with your heart-meltingly sweet housemate,' Maddie told Millie.

'Ooh, family takeaway! You enjoy that. Goodbye, Maddie,' Millie replied.

When she looked up from her phone, Millie saw Floyd was returning.

'Aw, you've discovered my Disney collection!' Floyd cried.

'Yes, and I have something to say about that,' Millie replied, pouting and glowering.

The tone of Millie's voice and her expression reminded Floyd of Dani's reaction to the revelation he read romance novels.

'It's bigger than mine! How dare you have more films than me? You even have *Beauty and the Beast* with Emma Watson. I've not got that one yet,' Millie complained.

When he realised Millie was just jealous, Floyd grinned. 'In my defence, I've trawled charity shops for *years* to build up this collection,' he pointed out.

'That's what I do too! Why pay full price when you can just give a pound to charity!' Millie cried.

'Absolutely, although DVDs and books are more than just a quid in some charity shops now,' Floyd agreed.

As the copy of *Frozen* he'd bought from The Salvation Army was in the player displaying its main menu, Floyd suggested: 'Shall we watch this? We can pause for me to dish up.'

'Yes,' Millie agreed.

A few moments later, Floyd found himself on the sofa with Millie and her blanket.

~

When the pasta dish he'd made for himself and Millie was cooked, Floyd paused *Frozen* and slopped it into bowls. The bowls weren't made for pasta, but it didn't stop them holding the warm and comforting food.

'I never asked what you got up to when I was at Maddie's birthday party? You said you were out at night,' Millie asked.

'I went on a date,' Floyd revealed.

That disappointed Millie. She wasn't sure why. 'Oh,' she whispered.

'Yeah, I think that word sums up my date,' Floyd said whilst transferring half the saucepan into a bowl.

'So you didn't fall head over heels for her?' Millie questioned.

'No. I remained upright, physically and metaphorically, as did she, despite her shiny white stilettoes,' Floyd told Millie.

The disappointment Millie had felt a moment ago was gone. 'White stilettos? Uncomfortable choice, though not uncommon in these parts,' she commented.

'Dani was the Essex girl stereotype come to life. Stilettos, fake tan, thick accent, the works. At home she's got a Chihuahua, who she sometimes carries in her handbag, and she called the food amazeballs,' Floyd revealed.

Millie giggled. 'Shut up!' she cried.

'Yeah, she said that too. All these years of dating and this is the first time I've seen someone who actually matches the stereotype,' Floyd told Millie.

'I can't believe there are people who think every female in the county is like that,' Millie said.

'I know. It must be hard for clever Essex girls like you,' Floyd replied.

As the food was done and she agreed with Floyd, Millie returned to the lounge with him and pasta. They sat some distance apart whilst eating and watching *Frozen*.

-

As soon as food was finished and Floyd had taken the bowls away, Millie sidled up to him again and wrapped them once more in the blanket together.

In the last part of the film, Floyd felt an odd sensation on his shoulder. He realised it was Millie. She had fallen asleep on him.

When the film ended, Floyd used his left arm very gently to get the remote and make it play again. He didn't want to disturb Millie.

At the part of *Frozen* when Elsa builds her ice castle, Millie started mumbling. She then sat up. 'What?' she questioned.

'You fell asleep, so I played it again,' Floyd explained.

As it dawned on her what had happened, Millie suddenly felt wide awake. 'Oh, I fell asleep on you! I'm so sorry!' she cried.

Floyd smiled. 'It's fine. You had a late one last night, so you needed the rest,' he said.

'I fell asleep on you,' Millie repeated.

'Yes, but I was cosy and toasty, so it was alright,' Floyd assured Millie.

'*Snuggly* and toasty. That's what I said,' Millie corrected.

'Yes, you did,' Floyd agreed.

To stop it babbling away to itself, Floyd paused the telly.

'It was a really good sleep. You have a very plumpfy shoulder,' Millie told Floyd.

'Thanks, I think?' Floyd replied.

Millie giggled. 'It means it is plump, good for resting my head on. That's probably because of my hoodie that you're still wearing. Sorry for confuzzling you,' she explained.

'Yes, I really should give the hoodie back,' Floyd said.

To return the item he'd stolen from her to Millie, Floyd got up and pulled her hoodie over his head. He accidentally caught his t-shirt as well.

For a few tantalising seconds, Millie was treated to a view of Floyd's torso. It wasn't particularly muscular or hairy. The blandness of it drew her toward it. Her hand stroked his bare skin. Sparks of electricity seemed to greet her fingertips. When she realised what she'd done, she grabbed the hem of Floyd's t-shirt and pulled it down.

'Thanks for that,' Floyd mumbled.

'It's fine,' Millie grinned.

After handing Millie her jumper, Floyd said: 'You can take that up to bed. I think that's us done for the night.'

As if to agree with Floyd, Millie yawned. 'I guess. Okay, then. Goodnight, Floyd,' she agreed.

'Night, Millie. I'll be up in a few minutes,' Floyd replied.

Taking the hint, Millie trundled up to bed. On the way, she whipped Floyd's hoodie off to return it to its home and put hers on, even though she was going to get undressed in a minute. It was warm because it had just been worn, which kept her snuggly and toasty on her way to bed, or *cosy* and toasty, as Floyd would say.

15

Chapter Fifteen

'Oh, *you're* the Christmas Genie!' Millie cried when the person she'd arranged to see joined her outside Holy Trinity Church.

Christmas Genie was a personal shopper service with a less dull title that helped people, today Millie, buy Christmas presents from the little shops along Colchester's Lanes. It turned out Eugenie, the cheery pink-haired woman who Millie had seen getting engaged just a few feet from where she was standing, was the one providing the service.

'Yes, me, Eugenie,' she confirmed.

'I saw your man propose to you outside this church. It was sweet,' Millie told Eugenie.

'Oh, that *was* sweet. He's such a romantic,' Eugenie replied dreamily.

Not wanting Eugenie to spend all her time daydreaming about her new fiancé, Millie asked: 'Have you had any ideas? On our call you said you'd use the information I'd given to work out what to buy my loved ones.'

Eugenie clapped her hands together excitedly. 'Ideas? I've had loads! Let's start with your bestie, Maddie,' she declared.

Bursting with energy, Eugenie bustled off down the street.

'It will be affordable, won't it?' Millie asked as she ran to keep up with Eugenie.

'Of course! I did take that on board!' Eugenie called back.

Old-fashioned lanterns hung off the buildings that lined the Lanes. The windows of the shops were full of glitter, gift ideas, and plush red fabrics. Christmas was in full swing for retail.

One shop had a mannequin sporting a long hot pink coat over chinos and a jumper standing next to a lit-up Christmas tree. Millie was able to admire this window, for Eugenie paused by it.

'I think we'll find something for Maddie inside,' Eugenie told Millie.

The pair headed into a little shop with plywood flooring. Their footsteps echoed in the compact interior. A woman behind the counter smiled at them, which made Millie feel warm and welcome.

'Hello, Auntie Victoria. Do you have the dress I asked for?' Eugenie asked the smiling woman.

It came as no surprise to Millie that the woman behind the counter was related to Eugenie. Cheeriness must be a family trait.

'It's in the stockroom. Just give me a minute, please,' Victoria replied.

'This is where I work when I'm not The Christmas Genie,' Eugenie revealed.

'Aw, a family shop. How sweet! Your aunt seems lovely,' Millie said.

'Thank you. She is *now*,' Eugenie agreed.

It only took Victoria a few seconds to locate the dress Eugenie had requested. When she brought the burgundy velvet number out, Millie gasped.

'You told me Maddie loves Disney. I think this dress is fit for a princess from one of the most famous recent films. This one is deep red, and the one in the film is green, but I think it works,' Eugenie explained.

'Anna! It's a Princess Anna dress!' Millie cried.

'So I'm told. I'm not a fan myself, but you're not the first to notice the resemblance,' Victoria commented as she laid the dress on the counter.

'Would Maddie like it?' Eugenie asked.

'Yes, but how can I afford it? This is a posh boutique. I can't shop in places like this,' Millie replied.

When she'd spoken, Millie had forgotten it was Eugenie's family shop. She felt a little guilty when she remembered. Eugenie wasn't posh.

'We're not *that* posh, definitely not *Pretty Woman* type posh. Add that this is heavily reduced because it has imperfections, and it's perfectly affordable,' Eugenie assured Millie.

'Oh, I want it. Maddie would love it,' Millie said.

'Then let's get it wrapped up,' Eugenie declared.

-

With a present for Maddie literally in the bag, Eugenie and Millie headed down the street. Eugenie was very mysterious, not telling her client where they were going. All she revealed was they were shopping for Millie's brothers and sister-in-law-to-be.

With Eugenie, Millie passed several clothing boutiques, an electrical store, a jeweller, some cafés, and various other businesses. It made her wonder what the Christmas Genie could possibly have in mind.

Eventually, Eugenie paused by a sweet shop. 'You mentioned that one of your fondest childhood memories was Jude sharing his pick and mix with you,' she said.

'Yes, I loved that. How did you remember?' Millie questioned.

'It's my job,' Eugenie replied with a smile.

To deny Millie the chance to praise her, Eugenie showed her client into the sweet shop.

'Yet more customers, Eugenie. This scheme is working wonders for us,' the man behind the counter commented.

'Your sweets make good presents. It's a pleasure to show them round,' Eugenie replied.

'Now I can buy Jude pick and mix to make up for all those times I snaffled his when we were kids,' Millie said.

Eugenie nodded. 'That's the idea,' she confirmed.

One wall was adorned with big transparent plastic tubs of sweets. Millie ordered various quantities of fizzy ones, sherbets, and citrus-flavoured sweets to make up a huge bag of unique pick and mix.

'Who did you say this was for?' the shopkeeper asked.

'Jude, my brother,' Millie told the shopkeeper.

'Okay. I'll just be a minute,' the shopkeeper replied.

After tying it up with a slim red ribbon, the shopkeeper took the bag away to a room Millie couldn't see. She could hear the whirring of a printer in the background.

A minute later, the shopkeeper brought the bag back. Stuck on it was a big orange sticker with "JUDE" printed in a bold black font.

'That's wonderful, thank you,' Millie said.

'Glad you like it. Anything else I can do?' the shopkeeper asked.

At one end of the wall of sweets were tubs of individually-wrapped chocolates. That reminded her it wasn't just Jude she was there to buy for.

'I'd like some raspberry ruffles and violet creams for Cecilia, my sister-in-law-to-be, please. A similar amount to Jude's bag,' Millie told the shopkeeper.

'Not a problem,' the shopkeeper replied.

-

Soon, Millie had two big, labelled bags of sweets, a bar of 90% cocoa dark chocolate, and still had money in her bank account.

'Now then, let's get a present for your parents,' Eugenie declared.

By now, Millie had learned not to ask her guide where they were going. It was more fun just to follow her cluelessly anyway. Eugenie knew what she was doing, and that was enough for Millie.

What Eugenie did this time was take Millie to an art shop. The crisp, tasteful appearance of the interior made Millie uneasy. She didn't think she could afford anything in there.

'Hi, Suzi! I'm after Josies Crafts!' Eugenie called.

As there were no other people in the shop, Millie wasn't sure who Eugenie was talking to.

A woman suddenly emerged from a door Millie hadn't noticed. 'Hello. I'll find them for you. I know they're here somewhere,' Suzi replied.

As swiftly as she'd appeared, Suzi disappeared through the same door.

'Josies Crafts?' Millie questioned.

'Handmade Christmas decorations,' Eugenie explained.

'Aw, how sweet! Mum and Dad will love them,' Millie said.

A lot of noise came from the stockroom, but Suzi didn't emerge with Christmas decorations.

'Do you think she's okay?' Millie asked.

'Yes, this is what Suzi is like. She's chaotic and disorganised, but a brilliant artist and businesswoman,' Eugenie assured Millie.

Eventually, Suzi returned with a big cardboard box that she put on the counter. When she opened it up, Millie could see it contained carefully wrapped bundles.

'It's good to get this box out. I really ought to display this lot,' Suzi commented as she unloaded the box she was referring to.

One of things Suzi removed that wasn't wrapped reminded Millie of the paper chains she'd made when she was little. Those chains had often fallen apart before Christmas Day. The chain Suzi held wasn't made of paper though. It looked like some kind of fabric.

'This is pretty,' Millie said, holding a length of the chain that had caught her eye.

'I like that too. It's a ribbon chain. Like a paper chain, but it's prettier and will last longer,' Suzi revealed.

'I want them. I want lots of them,' Millie declared.

With a smile, Suzi told her: 'That can be arranged.'

~

It transpired Suzi was correct. Millie was able to buy several metres of ribbon chain for her parents. She happily took it out of the art shop in a nice paper bag.

'Now we have presents for everyone you told me about. Is there anyone else you'd like to buy for?' Eugenie asked.

'Floyd,' Millie realised out loud.

A smile spread across Eugenie's face. 'Aw, your voice was so sweet then. I think I know the answer, but who is Floyd to you?' Eugenie replied.

'My housemate,' Millie told Eugenie.

The smile on Eugenie's face turned upside down. 'Oh, right,' she whispered.

Suddenly it dawned on Millie what Eugenie had thought. 'Did you expect me to say he's my boyfriend?' she questioned.

'Honestly? Yes. You said his name with such affection,' Eugenie admitted.

'He hasn't shown me any interest, at least not of the kissy-cuddly sort. Until now, I didn't think *I* had kissy-cuddly interest in *him*,' Millie replied.

'But you do have… Kissy-cuddly interest in him?' Eugenie enquired.

'Yes. I think I do,' Millie revealed.

'Then tell him! He might just be shy!' Eugenie cried.

'He might be,' Millie agreed.

This seemed to cheer Eugenie up. She put her arm around

Millie's and grinned at her. 'Right. Shall we get the man you have kissy-cuddly interest in a present?' she suggested.

'Yes!' Millie declared.

With their arms linked, Millie and Eugenie skipped along the lane, laughing as they went.

After almost a minute of gleefully traveling up one of Colchester's Lanes, Eugenie brought herself and Millie to an abrupt halt. 'I don't know where we're going! What does Floyd want?' Eugenie questioned.

'Books. Romance books,' Millie blurted out, as it was the first thing to come into her head.

'Great! Let's go to the bookshop. Jo can help us find a nice romance book for your Floyd,' Eugenie declared.

Together, Millie and Eugenie skipped a U-turn and headed back up the Lanes to the High Street.

16

Chapter Sixteen

Having lived with him for a little over a week, Millie knew roughly what time Floyd got back from work. Having bought a present for him, Millie wanted to get up to her room before he got home.

Happily for her, Floyd wasn't home when Millie got back from shopping with Eugenie. She was able to head straight up to her room without having her motives questioned.

As her room was quite small, Millie decided it would be best to put her presents under the bed. To check there was enough space as her suitcases were already there, she laid on the floor and had a peek. There was something there besides her suitcases. Curious, Millie stuck a hand in and pulled out a pair of briefs.

'Why?' Millie questioned, looking at the pants in her hands.

Whilst Millie was wondering why there was a pair of pants under her bed, she heard the front door slam. Floyd was home.

'Are you in, Millie?' Floyd called from downstairs.

'In my room. I'll be down in a minute!' Millie yelled back.

Once she'd safely stowed away her presents, Millie took herself and the pants she'd found down to the lounge.

'Ah, sorry. I obviously missed something. Where were they?' Floyd asked when he saw what was in Millie's hand.

'Under my bed, right against the wall,' Millie revealed.

Floyd shook his head. 'That room was a tip when he left it. I should have known I'd missed something. Sorry, Millie. It's not a nice thing to find,' he said.

'Oh, don't worry. I touched plenty of strangers' pants in my time. I was just curious. You are so houseproud and tidy. It seemed odd that there were dirty pants lying around,' Millie replied.

Whilst Millie took the pants to the kitchen to throw them away, Floyd wondered why Millie had touched "plenty" of strangers' pants. He wondered if she'd worked part-time in a lingerie shop to supplement her income.

Upon her return, Millie sat down next to Floyd on the sofa. As the boiler had been fixed, she didn't snuggle up under a blanket with him.

'Those pants you were unfortunate enough to find would have belonged to my ex-housemate,' Floyd explained.

When he saw the horrified look on Millie's face, Floyd realised what she thought he meant and laughed. 'No, not Jude. Not *that* ex-housemate. You didn't pick up your brother's dirty pants. I meant the guy after him,' he clarified.

'Oh, I see. He was untidy then?' Millie asked.

'He was lazy, which lead to untidiness, as well as many other things. He was a terrible housemate,' Floyd replied.

As she was thinking of her own terrible housemate, Millie only nodded in reply.

'He ate my food, he'd leave dirty things all around the kitchen for me to tidy up, and he even tricked me into doing his housework! After living with Jude, who was just a mate really, it was such a shock. I was *so* pleased to get rid of him, but also terrified that I'd end up replacing him with someone similar. That's why I jumped at the chance to have you here. The way Jude spoke about you, I knew you couldn't be like that last guy,' Floyd told Millie.

'That is bad luck, to end up with someone like that,' Millie sympathised.

It suddenly occurred to Floyd that, as a uni student, Millie probably had housemates back in Cambridge. 'Sorry for moaning. You must have seen it all, living with *students*,' he said.

'My *first* house was lovely and clean. We were all organised and respectful. There was even a rota for sharing jobs,' Millie revealed.

'*Very* nice. I'm guessing that's not the case now,' Floyd replied.

When Millie hesitated, something occurred to Floyd. 'Oh, is that why Maddie is always messaging? Gosh, I was so wrong. Maddie isn't a friend, is she? She's a bully, and she messages all the time to harass you,' he realised out loud.

Millie gasped. 'How can you think that?! *Maddie* isn't a bully!' she cried.

The emphasis on Maddie's name caught Floyd's attention. It was then he knew he'd unearthed something important. '*Maddie* isn't? Okay, who is?' he questioned.

'I never said anyone was bullying me,' Millie swiftly replied.

'Yes, that's true. *Is* someone bullying you, Millie?' Floyd asked.

Suddenly Millie found she couldn't look into Floyd's brown eyes. She gazed down at the floorboards.

'Millie? It's okay. You can tell me,' Floyd assured her.

'But I'm an adult. It's silly,' Millie mumbled at the floor.

When Floyd put a hand on her shoulder, Millie looked up at him. 'I'm here for you, Millie. Please tell me, or if you won't, at least tell Jude,' he begged.

'But it's really nothing,' Millie protested.

'If it's nothing, why is this making you so uncomfortable?' Floyd questioned.

'She just says not nice things, like I'm fat, or stupid, silly little nonsense like that. At the birthday party earlier this week, I sang *Let It Go* with Maddie very cheerily. She said that was childish, as was me being hurt by what she says,' Millie revealed.

'*I* think it's childish to say mean things about someone. That's playground behaviour,' Floyd pointed out.

As she'd never thought about it like that, Millie fell silent to consider Floyd's words.

'You don't have to put up with this, Millie. You certainly don't have to keep it to yourself,' Floyd told her.

'But it's silly! I'm an adult and I'm getting upset because a judgy girl says mean things to me,' Millie said.

'It's not silly. Her words are designed to hurt you. It's okay to admit that they do. Well done for telling me,' Floyd replied.

Sometimes, when laying in bed trying to sleep, Millie had had nightmarish daydreams in which she told someone how Kayleigh treated her. In her imagination, the person she'd told had laughed at her and told her to grow up. Not once had she imagined someone would praise her for admitting how much Kayleigh's nastiness hurt.

'You're so nice! You're the most un-Kayleigh housemate in the world,' Millie squeaked. Her voice was surprisingly weak.

When Floyd scooched up the sofa and wrapped Millie up in his arms, she realised she was crying.

'Sorry for being a cry-baby,' Millie wailed whilst crying.

Floyd stroked a hand through Millie's hair. 'You're not a cry-baby. It's okay. Let it out,' he whispered to her.

Being comforted by Floyd confirmed to Millie she wasn't a cry-baby. It also confirmed she was attracted to him.

-

When Millie's tears stopped flowing, Floyd released her and said: 'I'll be back in a minute.'

Without telling her what he was going to get, Floyd left Millie alone in the lounge and headed upstairs. Sitting by herself on the sofa, she wondered if she'd scared him. She didn't think she showed the full depth of her emotions often, and she could appreciate it was a lot to take.

When Floyd returned, he told Millie: 'I've got a couple of things for you.'

Once he'd sat down, Floyd handed Millie a tissue, so she guessed that was one of the things he had for her. She used it to wipe her face and then blow her nose. It felt as if that was the end of her releasing unhappy feelings. They were done with, for now at least.

The next thing Floyd gave Millie was a wooden keyring that had had the name "Millie" burnt into it with a pyrography pen.

As she stroked the wood of her new keyring with her thumb, Millie pointed out: 'But I already have one of these.'

'Yes, but I misspelt your name. That made it seem like not such a nice gift, so I had it redone,' Floyd explained.

'This, and flowers in my room on moving day, made me feel fuzzy inside and welcome. You are so sweet,' Millie told Floyd.

When Millie called him sweet, Floyd felt fuzzy inside. He couldn't even answer her.

The way Floyd was blushing and avoiding her gaze made Millie love him even more. He was too modest to take a compliment. At some point, she knew she'd have to reveal her feelings. This wasn't that some point. This was the some point to have dinner.

Millie didn't intend to keep her feelings hidden forever, but did so for the rest of the day.

17

Chapter Seventeen

Over hot, buttery toast he'd made, Floyd had told Millie they were going into town that evening. He'd advised her to wrap up warm, but that's all he'd said. When she'd asked for specifics, he'd just smiled at her.

During the day, Millie found it hard to focus on her book about a British woman who'd campaigned for boys and girls to receive an equal education. Though the subject of her book was fascinating and an important part of history and her university course, Millie couldn't help but wonder where she'd be spending her evening.

When Floyd got back from work and announced they'd be heading straight into town, Millie almost squealed with excitement. She wouldn't have to wait much longer.

On their way to do whatever is was they were doing that evening, Millie noticed Floyd walked between her and the road. He swapped sides when they crossed to continue to keep her on the inside. It was something she'd seen him do on their previous walks, but now she was sure it was deliberate. Though she thought it strange, she didn't comment on it.

Above the noise of traffic, Floyd heard Millie's tummy rumble. 'Don't worry. We'll treat ourselves to a takeaway after the activity,' he assured her.

'Activity? Whatever do you mean?' Millie asked.

Floyd smiled at his companion. 'You'll find out when we get there,' he answered.

When Millie realised she and Floyd were wandering up the road to the art gallery, she was a little disappointed. Art didn't interest her.

A poster caught Millie's eye. When she read the big letters on it, she gasped in delight. Now it made sense why Floyd had brought her there.

'Okay, the surprise is out now. We're going…' Floyd began.

'Ice skating!' Millie squealed, cutting Floyd off.

After she'd shrieked over Floyd, it occurred to Millie they may not in fact be going ice skating. A crushing sense of disappointment settled on her.

'We'll only get forty-five minutes on the rink, and it's synthetic, but it will still be fun,' Floyd told Millie.

This confirmation they would be ice skating sent Millie's spirits soaring. 'I've wanted to try ice skating for years, but never actually done it. Thank you so, so, much!' she replied.

Floyd shrugged. 'You're welcome. I went skating for my twenty-first and loved it, but haven't been on the ice since, so I'm quite excited too,' he said.

~

A few minutes after realising it was her destination, Millie was on the ice rink with Floyd. It only took a few seconds to realise she had questionable balance.

Balance didn't seem to be an issue for Floyd. He glided across the synthetic ice with ease, completing a full circuit before Millie had even made it ten feet from the entrance. When he noticed Millie wasn't as competent a skater as him, he returned to her side.

'Look at you go, show off!' Millie cried.

'Sorry for abandoning you,' Floyd said.

'It's fine. You were *amazing*!' Millie told Floyd.

'Thanks,' Floyd replied.

With one hand ready to grip the wall, and the other one holding Floyd's, Millie felt comfortable to complete circuit after circuit. She shared smiles with all the other skaters who wouldn't venture further than arm's length from the wall.

The way she moved on the synthetic ice made Millie feel like someone had cast a spell on her. In reality it was science, not magic, that made the surface and her movements on it special, but that wasn't how it felt to her. The freedom she was experiencing brought to mind fairies, not clever people in a lab trying to replicate the properties of ice.

With freedom in mind, Millie told Floyd: 'You must go off on your own again before our time is up.'

'But I'm here with you,' Floyd pointed out.

'Yes, but that doesn't mean we have to be together for all of it. Your solo skating was so good,' Millie replied.

As he'd enjoyed solo skating, Floyd didn't argue.

-

There wasn't much conversation between Millie and Floyd. Skating was entertaining enough for both of them.

When he thought there was about ten minutes left, Floyd broke the silence to say: 'I'm going to skate a bit faster now. Remember to glide and pivot.'

'Enjoy showoffy slippy-sliding!' Millie replied.

Just as he'd said he would, Floyd moved away from Millie and sped up, overtaking the skaters in front of them.

To Millie, there was something mesmerising about the way Floyd skated. He wasn't doing any tricks, partly because they weren't allowed, partly because he wasn't skilled enough to do them, but still he held her attention.

As he was paying full attention to what was in front of him, Floyd didn't notice Millie watching him.

As she was paying full attention to Floyd, Millie didn't notice she was catching up to the skater in front. She only knew they were there when she skated straight into her, knocking them into the wall and herself down onto the synthetic ice.

When they'd handed over her skates, a member of staff had told Millie not to put her hands out if she fell. She remembered this advice and crossed her arms.

'Are you alright?' asked the woman who Millie had skated straight into.

'She'll be fine, with all that padding,' someone with the woman replied before Millie had had a chance to answer.

'How dare you?! She's not fat. Millie is curvy, voluptuous, womanly, and beautiful on the inside, but not fat,' Floyd growled at them, having caught back up with Millie.

From the floor she was still laying on, Millie pointed out: 'Floyd, I skated into this person's friend. My fault.'

'And I didn't call her fat. I wouldn't do that,' the person Floyd had growled at added.

'Ah, yes. Sorry,' Floyd apologised.

The person who Millie had bumped into and her companion skated away, shaking their heads, leaving her to haul herself upright.

'Oh, I made a mess of that, didn't I?' Floyd groaned as he and Millie resumed skating around the edge of the rink, some way behind the people they'd spoken to.

'You were very protective of me. That person did comment on

my appearance, which is rude. They have no right to do that,' Millie replied.

Those were the last words to pass between them whilst they were on the ice rink. This didn't bother Millie though. Floyd had said more than enough.

18

Chapter Eighteen

'I hope this is good enough for you,' Floyd said to Millie as he led her into a chain burger joint.

'I love this place! I much prefer it to Maccy D's!' Millie cried.

The joy in Millie's voice made Floyd smile.

As it was close to Christmas and it was on the High Street, the burger joint was busy. The queue to the counter was long, and the narrow restaurant felt crowded.

When he realised people passing the queue as they left the restaurant may bump into Millie, as they had to some other waiting customers, Floyd swapped sides with her.

Once they had their food, Millie and Floyd made their way to one of the available tables. As Millie sat on the bench against the wall, Floyd couldn't pull her chair out. The food was in two brown paper bags. Floyd handed Millie the one containing her chicken burger, brushing her eagerly outstretched hand in the process. Instead of taking her bag and letting Floyd go, Millie grasped his hand and looked straight into his brown eyes.

'Floyd, there's something I want to ask you,' Millie told him.

The words, and the accompanying squeeze of Floyd soft, smooth hand, were meticulously planned. Millie had been dreaming about that moment for the entire walk from the ice rink to the burger joint.

'Okay, go ahead,' Floyd replied.

'I don't want you to think about your answer. It should come from the heart. Truthiness matters to me,' Millie told Floyd.

Floyd smiled. 'Okay,' he repeated.

'Did you mean what you said about me at the ice rink? Am I curvy, voluptuous, womanly, and beautiful on the inside?' Millie asked.

Millie remembering his speech word for word shocked Floyd, as did the question she asked. Her request for "truthiness" made him answer: 'Yes. I meant every word. You are all of those things.'

'Yay! That's what I was hoping you'd say. I have feelings for you too. You're heart-meltingly sweet, and kind, and warm, and caring, and thoughtful, and really handsome. This is wonderful!' Millie cried.

'Whoa, girl! Hold your horses! You're Jude's sister. I can't date you! That friendship is too precious to risk,' Floyd pointed out.

Millie snorted. 'Really? Jude is casual. He's hardly going to kick your door in and beat you up when he finds out,' she pointed out.

To give Floyd time to think about this, Millie removed her burger from its paper bag, unwrapped it, and took a bite. Her mouth watered when she tasted the juicy chicken and crispy batter.

'That's true. Also, if you're The One, I can't let Jude stand in the way,' Floyd thought out loud.

'The One?' Millie questioned.

'Yes, The One I'm going to marry and spend the rest of my life with. That's what I'm looking for, not a fling or a heartbreak. I want forever. If you're The One, no matter how scared I am of upsetting Jude, I'd have to date you,' Floyd explained.

'Aw! I can't believe you think I could be your forever partner. I'm touched,' Millie replied.

Floyd couldn't believe Millie hadn't laughed at his belief in The One. Most people he'd told about it mocked him. It seemed Millie shared his vision and was just as romantic as him.

'Whether or not we're life partners, we need to eat our food,' Floyd pointed out.

After giggling with pure glee, Millie had another bite of her chicken burger.

19

Chapter Nineteen

When Millie came downstairs in her pyjamas, Floyd smiled at her.

'It's Saturday, we're not going anywhere, and my sleepy clothes are *so* snuggly,' Millie explained.

'That's cool. All I'm wondering, although I think I know the answer, is what you want for breakfast?' Floyd replied.

'Toast, please. I'd love buttery, scrummy toast, which I could make for myself,' Millie told Floyd.

'You are so cute, and so not making toast. I'll do it for you,' Floyd said.

That was the first time Millie could remember being called cute by someone she wasn't related to. Her mum had called her cute throughout her childhood, and in her teens her oldest brother, Brandon, had told her she was infuriating but cute. Other people had used very different words to describe her, some of them far less sweet.

As she didn't have to make breakfast and was feeling lazy, Millie laid down on the sofa, grabbing a cushion to rest her head on. She curved herself around the corner to get comfortable. Even though she'd got more than eight hours of kip, she yawned and stretched.

~

The toast Floyd made her was every bit as scrummy as Millie had hoped it would be. She told him so after her first mouthful.

When he didn't have a mouthful of scrummy toast, Floyd asked: 'What do you want for the day?'

'Nothing. Absolutely nothing. Maddie's party was fun, but *exhausting*! I've spent the rest of the week studying hard. I think I've earned a day of rest and recuperation, which translates to laying on the sofa playing games or watching telly and scoffing biscuits,' Millie replied.

His housemate's wishes for the day made Floyd smile. 'Then that's what we shall do,' he declared.

The soulless chimes of the doorbell rang through the house. They were followed by the clatter of the door knocker.

'I interrupt this day of nothing to bring you unexpected guests at the door,' Floyd announced as if he was a news presenter.

Millie giggled. 'I'll answer. It's probably a door-to-door salesman. I love to keep them chatting for ages, asking silly questions, only to eventually tell them I have no money and these are not Chandler's pants,' she told Floyd.

The last thing Millie said made absolutely no sense to Floyd, but he let her go anyway.

When Millie opened the door, she found Cecilia standing there. As she knew her and Cecilia didn't have any encyclopaedias, Millie guessed she wasn't going to sell her anything.

'Tamsyn and I are off to the beach. We thought you might like to join us,' Cecilia explained.

The open door was allowing warm air to escape the house. To put an end to this, Millie stepped outside and shut it behind her. Doing so reminded her it was winter.

To remind Cecilia of the weather, Millie said: 'But it's cold outside.'

'It's hardly up to your knees out here,' Cecilia pointed out.

'Floyd will miss me, and I'm in sleepy clothes,' Millie realised out loud.

'It takes just a few minutes to change, and Floyd lives with you. I'm sure he can spare you for a little beach walk, unless you had plans,' Cecilia replied.

Ever since they'd first met, Millie had felt desperate to please Cecilia. Her blue eyes were pleading with Millie to come. She couldn't break their spell.

'Okay, thank you. I'll come to the beach with you. Let me just pop in to tell Floyd and get dressed,' Millie agreed.

-

On the drive to the coast, strong winds buffeted the car. Despite the speed limit being 60mph on the A133, Cecilia took it easy. The gusts were trying to take her little Mini off the road.

Thanks to careful driving, Cecilia made it to Frinton-On-Sea safely. There were many parking spaces along The Esplanade.

'It's not busy today,' Tamsyn commented.

'Of course not! Have you looked out the window? Who would walk on the beach on a day like this,' Millie cried.

Tamsyn cackled. 'Us, that's who. I grew up by the sea. There weren't many days I didn't head down to the beach, even in the depths of winter,' she replied.

Once Cecilia had reversed into a space, she pulled the handbrake on and switched the engine off. The wind howled around the car.

'Are we really going to do this?' Millie questioned.

'Yes. This isn't a dangerous storm,' Cecilia calmly confirmed.

With no way to get out of it, Millie pushed her door against the wind and got out the car. Once she had shut the door and zipped her coat up, she found it wasn't as bad as she'd thought. She was toasty, and she wasn't having to fight the wind like a mime artist.

Unlike Millie, Tamsyn practically jumped out the car. She inhaled the sea air and released a happy sigh.

'To the beach!' Cecilia declared.

Much to Millie's surprise, herself, Cecilia, and Tamsyn weren't the only people on the beach. There was a couple wandering in the opposite direction with their Labradors.

Fierce waves crashed onto the beach. They roared with the wind.

'I love a rough sea,' Tamsyn commented.

'Does it remind you of home?' Millie asked.

'Essex is home. The sea, especially when it's rough, reminds me of the best parts of Cornwall, where I grew up. I used to take my books to the beach when I was doing my A-Level's and dream of escaping to university,' Tamsyn replied.

An incoming wave progressed further up the sands than Millie had expected. She ran away from the sea shrieking, only just managing to keep her boots dry.

'Silly-wavey!' Millie cried as she ran.

Tamsyn cackled. 'That happened to me a lot when I lived in Cornwall, only I didn't always get away,' she admitted.

'I'm glad I escaped. I can't afford to ruin these boots. They were a gift from Maddie and I'm not sure of their waterproofyness. My student loan doesn't pay enough to replace them,' Millie said.

'Yes, it doesn't go far. I remember that from *my* uni years. My family didn't offer to help, and I wouldn't have taken anything from them anyway. I managed, but student life was tough,' Tamsyn agreed.

Knowing that Tamsyn had, like her, run away from waves and been a poor student, comforted Millie. Sometimes she wondered if she was the only person to struggle like she did.

'Was the struggle worth it though? Is your life better because you have a degree?' Millie asked.

'It is *so* much better. Apart from friendships, my job is the best part of my life, by far. I love it! Yes, uni was tough, as is my job, but I don't regret it for a second,' Tamsyn enthused.

'Glad to hear it,' Millie said.

The wind calmed and the waves began to lap at the sands rather than crash onto them. As she walked, Millie focused on the calming sound of the water moving in and out, in and out.

It wasn't just Millie who was listening to the waves. Tamsyn was too, though they were stressing her, not calming her. 'I really need a wee. Sorry,' she announced.

'That's okay. One of the many reasons I love Frinton is it has plenty of public conveniences by the beach,' Cecilia replied.

So Tamsyn could relieve herself, Cecilia led her and Millie off the beach to one of the public conveniences she'd mentioned. The building, with the pale-yellow render and gently sloping roof, was rather grand.

When Tamsyn's eyes saw the sign for the ladies, she felt even more desperate to use the facilities. To her despair, there was also a sign informing anyone who read it they'd need 20p to access the toilet. 'It needs a coin,' she whined.

Cecilia already had a hand in her bag. She pulled out a little black purse, which she unzipped. From that she produced a twenty pence piece, which she handed to Tamsyn.

'Thank you!' Tamsyn called over her shoulder as she dashed to the loos.

Only Cecilia and Millie were loitering around the public toilets. There were people in sight driving cars up and down the Esplanade, but no-one in earshot.

'I don't suppose you've been to the beach in a while, as there isn't one near Cambridge. What have you been up to?' Cecilia asked.

'Nothing, definitely not what you're thinking. I've been a good girl since you gave me a talking to. I don't do that anymore. I'm practically a nun these days,' Millie replied.

Cecilia frowned. 'That's not what I meant,' she said.

'Then what *did* you mean? You asked that question with some sort of meaning,' Millie questioned.

Cecilia hadn't intended Millie to know she'd asked her question with a particular meaning. She kicked herself for being so obvious. Now there was nothing she could do except explain herself. 'Jude and I have been worried about you. You returned to Essex early, desperate not to go back to Cambridge, and wouldn't tell us why. If you detected a hidden meaning in my question, it was just concern for you,' Cecilia explained.

Having used the toilet, Tamsyn came out wiping her hands on her jeans. 'Stupid hand dryer doesn't dry hands,' she muttered to herself.

Now Tamsyn had returned, Cecilia expected her conversation with Millie was over. She had failed in her mission to discover what was going on in her life.

'One of my housemates is a bully. Kayleigh says silly mean things, like children do. She's staying in Cambridge for the holidays, at least until Christmas Day itself, but Maddie went home as soon as term ended to get ready for her uncle's wedding, and she only returned to Cambridge for her birthday party. I know what Kayleigh says is nonsense, I'm not stupid, or fat, or any of the things she calls me, but it still upsets me. I couldn't bear her insults without the joy of seeing Maddie. That's why I ran home unexpectedly,' Millie revealed.

It amazed Millie she was able to talk about it, and so matter-of-factly too. She credited Floyd for helping her realise it wasn't her fault.

'Oh, Millie! Why didn't you tell us?' Cecilia asked.

'I was ashamed. It seemed so childish to be upset about it,' Millie explained.

'*You* have nothing to be ashamed of!' Cecilia cried.

The passion in Cecilia's voice made Millie smile. 'I know that now,' she told her.

The sea called to Tamsyn. She began to wander back to it, followed by Cecilia and Millie.

It was such a relief for Cecilia to know what had upset Millie. All she could think about as she returned to the beach was how Jude would feel when she told him what she'd discovered.

'Did I hear you're having issues with a housemate at university?' Tamsyn questioned.

'Yes,' Millie confirmed, wondering where that conversation was going.

'So did I. He wanted to date me, and was furious when I turned him down. He sniped at me for the rest of the term. It hurt me too. Nasty words can hurt. The next year though, I got my degree, moved into a long-term rental, and I've never seen him again. He's nothing to me now. I only remembered him because you talked about your housemate,' Tamsyn said.

'Oh, that's good to know,' Millie replied.

With sand under her soles again, Cecilia wondered if there was a way for Tamsyn and Millie to keep in touch. It seemed they had a lot in common.

As if to prove Cecilia's point, Millie and Tamsyn struck up a conversation about how people get bored when you discuss the details of the subject you love with them. Tamsyn described what she looked for on ECG and Millie listened intently. She was not bored at all, and neither was Cecilia.

20

Chapter Twenty

On a cold December Sunday, the walk into town felt rather long. Millie's legs begin to ache, and her cheeks chilled. It wasn't as windy as the beach at Frinton, so she carried on. If she could do that then she could walk into the city centre.

'Why won't you tell me where we're going?' Millie asked.

'Because it's a surprise!' Floyd cried for the fifth time that day.

It transpired the surprise was to take place in a grand red brick Victorian hotel. This surprised Millie. It didn't look like the sort of place she thought Floyd liked.

When Floyd pushed the door into the vast entrance hall, a smartly-dressed member of staff approached him. 'Can I help you, sir, madam?' they enquired.

'Yes, please. I have a booking for Christmas afternoon tea in the name of Floyd Kiernan,' Floyd told the member of staff.

The member of staff nodded. 'Of course, sir. Please come with me to the desk so I can locate the details of your booking and inform you where you are to be seated,' they replied.

As they'd been told to, Millie and Floyd made their way to the desk. Whilst she waited for the member of staff to type something, Millie fidgeted. The polished marble floor and spacious surroundings didn't make her feel comfortable.

'Ah, yes, Mr Kiernan. You are to take festive afternoon tea in The Rose Room. I shall take your coats and show you through,' the member of staff told Floyd.

As soon as she entered it, Millie could see why it was called The Rose Room. The walls were a deep pink and the light fittings on the chandeliers looked like roses. A roaring fire gave it a cosy and warm atmosphere.

'Wow,' Millie whispered.

'I must admit that I do rather like The Rose Room. Should I ever leave reception, I'd wish to work in here,' the member of staff confessed.

Another person in a waistcoat approached the member of staff who'd shown Millie and Floyd to The Rose Room. They smiled at Millie, which made her feel welcome.

'Good afternoon, Penny. Please look after Mr Floyd Kiernan and his companion. They are non-residents here for afternoon tea,' the member of staff from reception informed their colleague.

Once again, Penny smiled. 'My pleasure. Come this way, Mr Kiernan,' she said.

Penny led Millie and Floyd through the tables, which wasn't difficult as there was plenty of space between them, to an empty one for two by the fireplace. As soon as Penny gestured at the table, Floyd sprang forward and pulled out one of the chairs.

'Please be seated here. Your afternoon tea will be brought out shortly,' Penny told her guests.

'Great. Thanks for that,' Floyd replied.

As she sat down, Millie said: 'Aw, thank you.'

'You're welcome,' Floyd told Millie as he pushed her chair in.

Penny smiled at Floyd's behaviour. 'I'll be back soon with your tea,' she replied before leaving them to date in peace.

Once he'd sat down opposite Millie, Floyd asked: 'So, how are you feeling about our first date?'

'Fine. We already know each other,' Millie said.

'Ah, but a date is different. This is about finding out if we *love* each other,' Floyd pointed out.

'Well, I know you're sweet. When I moved in, you made me feel so welcome with my own keyring, flowers in my room, and your warm personality. Kindness is very loveable,' Millie told Floyd.

'And you're fun-loving and bubbly. Being with you makes the world brighter,' Floyd replied.

The words found their way to Millie's heart and touched it in a way it had never been touched before.

Much to Millie's delight, Penny came over at that moment with their tea on a tray. She placed the delicate bone china cups on the table along with a teapot, a petite jug of milk, a pot of sugar, and a couple of teaspoons. All the crockery matched.

'What's the funny metal thing?' Millie asked, pointing at something that had been placed across the top of her cup.

'That is a tea strainer. You pour the tea through it,' Penny explained.

'Oh, thank you. Sorry if I'm a silly-Millie for asking,' Millie apologised.

Penny flashed a grin at Millie. 'Not at all. Happy to help,' she replied.

Having helped, Penny headed off to assist someone else.

As she watched Penny walk away, Millie noticed how smartly-dressed everyone was. The trousers and blouse she'd put on that morning weren't scruffy, certainly not by her standards, but in them she felt out of place. It made her squirm in her seat.

'I am looking forward to the food,' Floyd said.

'Oh, yes! I love sweet treats, and am fascinated to see how they Christmasify it all,' Millie agreed.

'You are so cute,' Floyd told Millie.

Millie giggled. 'I'm just being me,' she replied.

'And that's what makes you so... Loveable, as you put it,' Floyd pointed out.

So cute and loveable Millie didn't get thirsty, Floyd picked up the teapot and carefully poured into her cup through the tea strainer. Once he'd returned the teapot to the table, he splashed a drop of milk into Millie's cup. Only then did he make himself a cup of tea. His cup contained sugar and more milk than Millie's.

When Millie went to pick her tea up, Floyd reminded her: 'It will be hot.'

'Oh, thank you. You can tell I'm studying philosophy, not temperaturey science,' Millie replied, putting the teacup back down.

Instead of telling Millie the word she was looking for was thermodynamics, Floyd smiled at her and stirred his tea.

As he was looking at Millie, Floyd didn't see Penny approaching with food. He did see Millie's face light up, so he knew it was coming.

In the centre of the table, Penny placed a cake stand that matched the teacups, saucers, and other crockery. It was adorned with shortbread in the shape of a Christmas tree, bite-sized scones with equally small glass pots of Tiptree preserve, sandwiches with fillings as yet unknown to Millie and Floyd, and many other sweet and savoury little treats.

Before Penny was even three steps away, Millie had picked up a finger sandwich. She scoffed it immediately. The noises Millie made told Floyd she liked the sandwich.

'What's in it?' Floyd asked.

Once she'd swallowed, Millie replied: 'Turkey and stuffing. It's a Christmas dinner sandwich.'

Whilst Millie ate a gingerbread man that had been iced to look like he was wearing a tuxedo, Floyd munched on a pig in blanket.

-

Eating festive afternoon tea caused a cessation of conversation. Millie and Floyd didn't mind this, as scoffing seasonal sweet and savoury treats was an all-consuming and immensely enjoyable experience.

When conversation resumed in the absence of festive afternoon tea, which had all been eaten, it turned to the cost of the food and drink they'd enjoyed so much.

'I dread to think how much this will all come to,' Millie commented.

'Don't worry about that. I've got this,' Floyd assured her.

As far as Millie knew, Floyd worked in a call centre. She had no idea how he could afford festive afternoon tea at a fancy hotel. It also confused Millie that Floyd had chosen to go somewhere so high-end. He came across as casual and understated, but their current surroundings were anything but.

It seemed Penny had sensed Millie was thinking about the bill, for she came over with it. 'How do you wish to pay?' the waitress asked.

Floyd reached into the pocket of his trousers and pulled out a sheet of paper. 'With this, please,' he replied, handing it to Penny.

Once she'd examined the paper, Penny said: 'Ah, a gift certificate. How marvellous. What a nice present someone gave you.'

'Yes, I am lucky. I could never have come here otherwise. As it is, I can't afford to leave a tip. Sorry,' Floyd told the waitress.

'There is no need for an apology. A tip is not required here,' Penny assured Floyd.

It saddened Millie that herself and Floyd couldn't afford to reward Penny's good service with money. 'You've been lovely, Penny. So warm, friendly, and helpful,' Millie enthused.

Like she had already done several times, Penny smiled. 'That is worth more to me than money, so thank you, madam. Those words shall stay with me far longer than a monetary tip would have done,' she replied.

Another diner waved their hand for Penny's attention, so she left Millie and Floyd's table.

'Shall we go?' Floyd asked.

'Yes,' Millie agreed, getting up.

-

On the walk home, Millie wondered something. When she and Floyd reached the gates to Castle Park, she decided to voice her thoughts. 'Who gave you a free afternoon tea at a fancy-pantsy hotel?' Millie asked.

'My supervisor. It was a reward for retaining the most customers,' Floyd explained.

In front of Millie and Floyd was the Norman keep Castle Park was named after. She stopped right by the bridge to the entrance. Floyd paused too, thinking that Millie was admiring the building. He was shocked when she turned away from the castle and placed her lips on his.

After a second or two, Millie removed her lips from Floyd's so she could use them to say: 'That was me congratulating you.'

In response, Floyd kissed Millie. It was softer than any kiss she'd ever experienced. He had a hand on her back, gently keeping her close. When she'd been kissed before, Millie had felt it as a fire down below. This kiss triggered a tingly warmth that spread from her lips to every part of her body. The reactions to previous kisses had been purely physical. She felt Floyd's kiss in her soul.

Much to Millie's dismay, Floyd didn't spend the rest of the day kissing her, or even the rest of the minute. He ended it to tell her: 'I'd hoped for a setting more romantic than the entrance to the park for our first kiss, but it was a spectacular kiss nonetheless.'

When Floyd's lips had connected with hers, Millie had been unaware of her surroundings. She hadn't cared then that she was in Castle Park, and she still didn't care. In a slightly perturbed tone, she replied: 'The moment felt right, and that matters more than the setting, not that I think outside the castle is a bad setting. You're handsome and loveable no matter where we are.'

21

Chapter Twenty-one

As the recipe told her to, Millie emptied some of the packet of flour into the bowl.

'I think that's too much,' Floyd commented.

'I'm sure it's fine,' Millie replied as she set the packet of flour down on the work surface.

'It doesn't look right,' Floyd argued.

When she looked at Floyd's frowning face, Millie knew what to do with the supposedly-excess flour in the bowl. She scooped some up with her hands and threw it at him.

'What?!' Floyd cried, staring at Millie.

Millie giggled. 'You said there was too much flour in the bowl. I was just taking some out,' she pointed out.

'A food fight? Seriously?' Floyd growled.

With her sweetest smile, Millie replied: 'I'm cute. You told me so. You can't be cross with a cute girl like me, can you?'

Floyd sighed. 'No, I'm not cross. Could you please get me the salt out of the cupboard at the end?' he requested.

Just like she'd been told to, Millie turned her back on Floyd to get the salt. He took this opportunity to take a handful of flour and throw it at her. It coated her blonde locks and made her shriek.

'Yeah, that's definitely the right amount of flour now,' Floyd said.

As she put the table salt in front of Floyd, Millie told him: 'You are evil.'

'You started it,' Floyd pointed out.

'Well, I shall end it by going off to have a shower,' Millie declared.

To do what she'd said she'd do, Millie began to head out of the kitchen.

'You go have a shower. That way we might actually end up with edible food,' Floyd said.

Millie paused her journey to the bathroom to spin round and glare at Floyd. 'I could always stay here and throw more flour at you,' she replied.

Whilst Floyd chuckled behind her, Millie strolled out of the room.

-

'Oh, mate, you're cooking? That's so nice. I only needed snacks or something,' Jude told Floyd when he stepped through the door and got a whiff of the food in the oven.

'Millie and I need dinner, so I thought I may as well make enough for you too,' Floyd pointed out.

Once he'd closed the front door, Floyd showed Jude through to the lounge. Jude's eye was drawn to the back of Floyd's head.

'Millie is just dishing up now,' Floyd revealed.

'That's cool. Did you know you got flour on you?' Jude asked.

As Jude asked his question, Millie walked into the room with two plates of toad in the hole.

'Oh, is it still there? I thought I'd got it off,' Floyd said, brushing a hand over his hair.

Jude and Floyd sat on the sofa so Millie could hand them their food. Jude couldn't help looking at the flour on Floyd's head again.

'We had a little food fight. That's why he's got flour on him. I had a shower to get it off me,' Millie explained.

Jude grinned. 'Oh, really? So you two threw flour at each other?' he questioned.

'Yes. It was silly fun. I loved seeing Floyd all messy,' Millie confirmed.

Floyd's eyes widened. 'It's just what *housemates* do, have food fights. Friends too, and that's what Millie and I are, housemates and friends,' he rapidly added.

As he was concentrating on Jude's reaction, Floyd didn't see the confusion on Millie's face. He was just pleased Jude accepted his words.

To get her own food, Millie returned to the kitchen. She remained in there for a moment, replaying the events of the last few days. As far as she knew, she and Floyd were now dating. That made them more than friends and housemates. What he'd said to Jude suggested she'd misunderstood. There was no denying their kiss outside the castle had been sizzling though. At that moment, she'd been in no doubt he loved her. Now it didn't seem so clear.

Unable to quiz Floyd in front of Jude, Millie just took her food to the front room and ate in silence.

-

Once food had been eaten, Floyd turned the Nintendo Wii on. Jude had come to game, and that was exactly what they were going to do.

'Do you want to join in, Millie? It can split the screen for three?' Floyd offered.

'Yeah, of course! Let's play!' Millie agreed, reaching to grab her remote before Floyd had even picked it up off the side to give to her.

'Has he got you onto this?' Jude asked.

'Yes! It's so fun!' Millie enthused.

'Floyd is seriously good at this though. It don't matter, cos it's the taking part that counts, but we don't stand a chance,' Jude said.

'I'm better! I beat him!' Millie proudly replied.

Jude raised an eyebrow but said nothing. He had a suspicion which he wasn't willing to voice.

Unlike when he'd played with just Millie, Floyd told the game to choose tracks at random.

When the countdown began, Millie focused in on her corner of the screen. It was all that mattered. The word "START" flashed up and Millie did so, pressing her thumb down hard on the button that served as the accelerator. A few seconds into the race, Millie realised the course was just a simple oval around a lake with three waterfalls gushing across the track. As she wasn't sure how strong the current of the water was, Millie used the bridges that crossed it to ensure she didn't end up in the lake. Some of her computer-controlled rivals had the same idea, but she weaved her way through them to get up to third place by the end of the first lap.

Far behind Millie was Jude. He was tailing Floyd, who got shoved into the water by a heavier kart. Jude seized the initiative and overtook him, something he was rarely able to do.

For the rest of the race, Jude cruised along in fifth, sometimes sixth position. He paid more attention to Millie and Floyd's portions of the screen than his own. He saw his sister take second place when the kart in front got shot by a shell. He also saw Floyd throw that shell, taking care to aim at the character that had been in front of Millie. Once behind Millie, instead of closing on her, Floyd made a beeline for a banana skin and ran over it, causing his kart to spin out.

At the end of the race, Millie was in first place. Floyd was only in fourth. 'Yay, I got the gold, and Floyd isn't even on the podium. Told you I was better than him,' she gloated.

'Yeah, you did,' Jude murmured.

'Well done, Millie. An excellent race,' Floyd said.

So eager was Millie to race that she held down the accelerator as soon as the countdown started. This meant her engine stalled and she was stuck on the line as everyone else raced past.

'No! I can't be last!' Millie cried.

In the two seconds or so she was stuck for, Millie let her attention drift to Floyd's part of the screen. She watched him weave all over the track, hitting every obstacle on the way. As she began to drive, Millie realised why Floyd was doing that. A feeling of rage more intense than the one she'd felt when she'd stalled the kart overcame her.

'You're letting me win. What are you doing that for?' Millie asked.

'No, Jude really is that bad,' Floyd told Millie.

'Not him, *you*. You are running over everything in your path,' Millie growled.

Having grown up with her, Jude knew to stay out of the row between Millie and Floyd. Her anger could be intense. On this occasion, he understood the cause of it.

'Well, I can't as a true gentleman beat a girl,' Floyd replied as he navigated a tricky bend.

By now, Millie had stopped racing. She'd parked her kart on the verge and put her controller down.

'Why?' Millie questioned.

When he tried to answer that question, Floyd stuttered. 'You're a girl,' he eventually replied.

'Yes, I know that. Why does that mean you should let me win at a video game?' Millie asked.

Not on purpose for once, Floyd crashed into the side of the track. 'Oh, for goodness sake! It was supposed to be nice!' he cried.

'But it *isn't* nice. It suggests I'm less capable than you on account of my sex,' Millie pointed out.

Whilst Floyd was desperately trying to work out how to reply, Millie stormed out of the room.

'Oh, I've really messed up,' Floyd groaned.

'Yeah, you have,' Jude agreed.

When Floyd's head fell into his hands, Jude told him: 'She'll calm down as quickly as she got cross. I'll go talk to her, which'll give you time to work out how to fix this.'

Up in her bedroom, Millie was sitting on the bed and staring at the wall. All the joy she'd felt playing Mario Kart with Floyd was tainted now. It made her question who he was. She thought she loved him, but she didn't love what he'd done.

'Is there a Miss Emily Cassandra Austen up here?' Jude asked as he entered his sister's room.

The use of her full name made Millie giggle. 'There's a Millie up here. Will that do?' she replied.

In response, Jude shut the door and sat down next to his sister.

'Am I silly to be cross at Floyd for letting me win?' Millie wondered out loud.

'Nah, not at all. It's what Floyd's like though. It ain't about you, little sis. When he dates a girl, he behaves like he's straight out of a period drama. He turns up all smart, pulls her chair out, lets her order first, *always* pays the bill, that sort of thing,' Jude revealed.

After wondering what period dramas Jude watched, Millie replied: 'But I like all the things you just mentioned. They make me feel special. Letting me win feels different. When he opens a door for me, I don't feel like he's doing it because I can't. Being deliberately rubbish at the game suggests that, if he played his best, I wouldn't win.'

'To be fair to him, Floyd has probably dated girls who would throw a hissy fit if beaten at a game. He's had some funny girlfriends. It probably hasn't occurred to him that you're not dating, and you're not like those girls he's known,' Jude pointed out.

'I hope you're right. I hate the idea of him not seeing me as an equal,' Millie replied.

Though Millie was a little upset, Jude was confident she and Floyd would patch things up. He'd never known her hold a grudge against anyone.

The concern Jude had felt for her reminded Millie of something. 'Sorry for making you all scaredy when I turned up on your doorstep at the start of the month,' she said.

'Oh, that's fine. It's just a big brother thing, worrying about your little sis. I were glad when Cecilia told me what were up. Thanks for telling her about it,' Jude replied.

'Thank Floyd. I told him first, and he helped me realise I wasn't the childish one, and I'd done nothing wrong. Because of that, I felt able to share with Cecilia, and also with Tamsyn, who is very cool,' Millie told Jude.

'I'm glad you and Floyd like each other. He's a decent guy, and was a great housemate,' Jude commented.

That compliment reinforced Millie's belief that Jude would be perfectly happy about the fact she'd fallen for Floyd. She was definitely happy to have fallen for him, and, after her chat with Jude, was looking forward to spending more time with him. She was also looking forward to seeing Jude again on Christmas Eve Eve.

22

Chapter Twenty-two

Every time Millie looked up from her book, her eyes were drawn to the cardboard box in the corner of the room, and then to the clock. One was full of Christmas decorations, and the other told her when Floyd would be back from his half day so they could put the Christmas decorations up together.

When it got to the time Floyd's shift ended, Millie put her book down and headed to the kitchen to make sandwiches. The sooner he was fed, the sooner they could decorate.

A few minutes after Millie had finished making sandwiches, the door opened. She picked up both plates and carried them through to the lounge, where Floyd was putting his bag down.

'Hello, cutie,' Floyd said.

'Lunch. Eat up,' Millie replied, thrusting one of the plates into Floyd's now-empty hands.

For a moment, this briskness confused Floyd. When he realised the cause, he smiled. 'Is someone eager to decorate the house by any chance?' he asked.

'More eating, less talking!' Millie ordered.

'You're a little scary right now,' Floyd replied.

As she was scoffing her sandwiches, Millie just glared at Floyd.

At last, Floyd took the hint and took a bite of his food, following Millie's lead.

-

To keep moody Millie at bay, Floyd wolfed down his sandwiches at the same rate she did, not even pausing to taste them. They were formed of the cheapest white bread, supermarket's own spread, and wafer-thin ham, so he didn't miss much.

As soon as it was empty, Millie snatched Floyd's plate off him and rushed it to the kitchen. When she returned to the lounge, she knelt down on the floor by the box of decorations and slapped her knees.

'You do know these aren't the finest decorations in the land? They don't even have a special family history. Jude and I picked them up at a car boot the first Christmas he was living with me,' Floyd told Millie as he joined her on the floor.

'To me, that *is* a special history. These are the Austen/Kiernan house decorations,' Millie replied.

'That should be Kiernan/Austen house. Officially, I'm the tenant,' Floyd said.

'I thought you were a believer in ladies first,' Millie pointed out.

'Yeah, that's true. You win. This is the Austen/Kiernan house,' Floyd conceded.

'Yay! My hours of debating at uni have paid off!' Millie cried.

'Ah, you are trained in the art of debate. No wonder I couldn't win,' Floyd replied.

Having lost a debate with Millie, Floyd opened the big box of Christmas decorations. The first thing he pulled out was a smaller and thinner box.

'This is our Christmas tree. It's three foot tall and pink,' Floyd told Millie.

As she took the box from Floyd, Millie looked at a picture of the tree on it. 'Ooh, it's cute,' she commented.

On his second delve into the box, Floyd retrieved a long strand of silver tinsel. It sparkled in the sunlight streaming in through the large front window. Once he'd liberated the whole strand of tinsel, he wrapped it around Millie.

'I'm not a Christmas tree!' Millie pointed out.

'Ah, sorry. You're cute, and so is our tree. I got confused,' Floyd apologised.

When Floyd went to remove the tinsel around her, Millie grabbed it and held it close to her. 'No, leave it. I like being Christmasifyed,' she told Floyd.

'Very well then,' Floyd replied.

With a smile on his face, Floyd grabbed a fairy tree topper from the box and placed it on Millie's head. She giggled, which almost dislodged the dainty fairy, but the decoration just about managed to stay on.

'I want to see how silly I look. Please may you take a picture of me?' Millie asked.

As requested, Floyd got up off the floor, picked his phone up off the side, and snapped a few photos of Millie wearing tinsel and a tree topper. She beamed at the camera. For the first time, Floyd noticed Millie had dimples.

So Millie could see her photos, Floyd decided to message them to her. He scrolled through his list of contacts until he got to one called "Austen, Millie" and sent the pictures to her.

When Millie's phone made a noise, Floyd told her: 'That will be the pics of you. I sent them for you to look at later.'

The tree topper fell off Millie's head, but it didn't matter. Floyd had already recorded the moment for her. She'd treasure those photos forever, maybe even get them printed one day.

'Now then, why don't you build the tree while I find suitable decorations?' Floyd suggested.

'Good plan,' Millie agreed.

As soon as Floyd had made his good plan, his phone rang. He got it out and took a look at the screen. 'I'll be back,' he murmured as he took the mobile phone and himself out of the room.

-

Within an hour the lounge had been, as Millie put it, "Christmasifyed". The pink tree sat on the edge of the TV stand adorned with miniature silver baubles, silver tinsel that looked huge wound around the short branches, and a little star on top. There was more tinsel on the walls, and battery-powered twinkling lights in the window above the fairy tree topper Millie had worn as a hat.

In the middle of the lounge, Millie was swaying from side to side and taking in her surroundings. 'It's beautiful!' she commented.

'So beautiful that you're dancing? Is that another cute thing you do? Do you dance when you see beautiful things?' Floyd questioned.

'No, I need a wee,' Millie explained.

'Then go. The room is decorated,' Floyd told Millie.

As she really was desperate, Millie dashed off to the toilet.

With the lounge to himself, Floyd made his way to the box and pulled out one of the many decorations he and Millie had decided not to use. It was something she hadn't seen. He'd hidden it behind other decorations.

Oblivious to what was going on in the lounge, Millie viewed the pictures of herself dressed up in tinsel and a tree topper. She laughed at them before sending one to Maddie.

After washing her hands, Millie read Maddie's almost-instantaneous response that asked what emoji the picture she'd just sent was supposed to represent.

Whilst telling Maddie her photo wasn't an emoji, just something silly she'd done with Floyd, Millie sauntered back into the lounge. Floyd was waiting for her, standing in the middle of the room. The way he was looking at her suggested he wanted something, but she wasn't sure what.

'Are you alright?' Millie asked Floyd as she returned her phone to its rightful place in her jeans pocket.

Floyd glanced above Millie's head and then back at her. When she frowned at him, he repeated the action.

'What?' Millie questioned, looking behind her at the door she'd just walked through. That's when she saw it. Above the door was fake mistletoe.

Now Millie was aware of what he'd done, Floyd took a step closer to her. 'It might not be real mistletoe, but I think we still should,' he said.

'I agree. We must smooch' Millie replied.

To stop Millie using them to talk, Floyd gently ran his index finger along Millie's lips. He held her gaze as he did this twice. Her grey eyes were full of anticipation. In one smooth motion, Floyd replaced his finger with his lips. The kiss lasted for a few seconds of tingles and togetherness. That was enough for the pair of them... for now.

23

Chapter Twenty-three

'We must have a tub of chocolates. It's Christmas!' Millie pleaded when Floyd attempted to walk past the confectionery aisle.

'And we're on a budget so we can enjoy other luxuries,' Floyd pointed out.

Whilst walking around the shop, Millie had held her phone in her hand. She'd been using the calculator to add up how much it would all come to as they went along. On another app, she had a shopping list. Most of the items on it had been ticked off.

'There's not much left to get, and we're cosily under budget. Please may we get a tub of chocolates?' Millie asked again.

When Floyd's gaze locked with Millie's, his resolve weakened. 'How can I say no to those sparkling grey eyes? Go and get your chocolates. I'll wait here, so as not to get tempted by the biscuits,' he replied.

With a squeal of happiness, Millie abandoned Floyd and the trolley to dance down an aisle in search of a cheap and cheerful chocolate tub.

There were several tubs of chocolates to choose from. As she wanted to be sure she'd got the best one, Millie lingered by the shelf, picking up each tub in turn and reading the contents.

'Millie? Is that you?' a voice behind her asked.

When Millie turned away from the chocolates, she found that she didn't recognise the man who'd spoken to her. 'I *am* Millie, but who are *you*?' she questioned.

Hurt crossed the man's face. 'Well, I guess it was dark, and I didn't have clothes on for most of the time we were together. Neither did you, but I'd recognise that arse anywhere,' he replied.

Though she still couldn't remember his name, Millie now knew how the man knew her.

'It's Gavin,' the man reminded Millie.

'Of course it is. What are you doing here?' Millie wondered out loud.

'I gave up on uni. Too much like hard work, and it didn't earn me a penny. I've got a job now, but I have to travel with it. This week it's brought me to Colchester, and to the sexiest girl in the world,' Gavin explained.

There were no questions in what Gavin had said, and Millie didn't find it interesting, so she saw no reason to answer.

'I'm in Colchester for just one more night. I've got myself a room at Bridge House Hotel, room one. Don't suppose you'd like to drop by tonight, around nine? We could have some fun, like we did that unforgettable night back in Cambridge,' Gavin suggested.

At the top of the aisle, Floyd had seen a man accost Millie. Judging by her body language, she wasn't happy to be talking to the man. Concerned for her, he decided to interrupt. He set off down the aisle with his trolley.

'I don't do that anymore,' Millie told Gavin.

Just as Floyd got close enough to hear, he heard the man who'd interrupted Millie say: 'Shame. You were bloody good in bed. You closing your legs is a tragedy for all mankind.'

Having realised he wasn't going to get what he wanted from her, Gavin left Millie to shop. She let out a breath she hadn't known she was holding.

'Who was that?' Floyd asked.

As Millie hadn't realised Floyd was there, she jumped when he spoke. 'Someone from Cambridge,' she swiftly replied.

'An ex-boyfriend,' Floyd concluded.

'Ex-*lover*,' Millie corrected.

Shoppers in search of bargains swarmed around Millie and Floyd. They weren't aware of their conversation. Floyd wasn't aware of them, but he was very aware of a word Millie had used.

'*Lover*?' Floyd questioned.

Gavin came from a part of Millie's life she hadn't wanted to share with Floyd. It now seemed like she didn't have a choice. She let that annoyance out in a sigh. 'I slept around a lot in my first year at Cambridge. Gavin was nothing more than a night's entertainment,' she explained.

Though there was a hubbub in the supermarket, Millie found Floyd's silence deafening. Second after second passed with no reply from him. Words weren't necessary for Millie to get the message.

'You were already ashamed of me. Now you're disgusted too,' Millie said.

'What?' Floyd questioned.

Every part of Millie had wished for Floyd to contradict her. She needed him to tell her he wasn't ashamed of her, and he wasn't disgusted. When he didn't, her heart crumbled.

'I don't need to be around judgy people!' Millie snapped.

Desperate for some space between her and Floyd, Millie stormed out of the shop. By the time she'd reached the car park, the world was blurry. She was sobbing.

Through a wall of tears, Millie found her way to the bus stop. She leaned on the pole and cried her eyes out. Her past had come back to bite her.

Over her loud sobs, Millie heard someone running towards her. She looked up and saw Floyd approaching. '*Why would he chase after me when he hates me?*' Millie wondered.

'Millie! What's going on? We need to get back to the shop to buy your chocolates!' Floyd cried.

'Buy me chocolates? Don't you hate me?' Millie questioned.

Floyd frowned. 'What sort of a question is that, and where did you get this idea that I'm ashamed of you? I adore you, Millie, and I couldn't be prouder to call you my girlfriend,' he replied.

'You don't hate me?' Millie whispered, emotion making her voice weak.

As it was the only way he could think of to assure Millie he didn't hate her, Floyd stepped forward and wrapped her up in a hug. He held her close, tight and warm. In his arms, he felt her settle. He heard her stop crying. The message was getting through.

'Why were you silent in the shop, and why did you tell Jude so vehemently that we're housemates?' Millie questioned, her breath soft against Floyd's shoulder.

So he could look Millie in the eye, Floyd let her go. 'Oh, is that where you got the idea that I'm ashamed of you? I didn't tell Jude about us because I'm scared. You're his beloved little sister. I'm not sure he'd like the idea of me dating you. As for in the shop, I was just so shocked. I thought you were a romantic, like me,' Floyd explained.

A crack in the pavement caught Millie's attention. 'Everyone else did it. When I caved to pressure, I found I enjoyed it. Sex is fun, and all those boys wanting me made me feel good,' she murmured.

'I want you Millie. I want your soul,' Floyd told her.

When Millie's eyes widened, Floyd commented: 'That sounded way creepier out loud than it did in my head.'

The light and bubbly sound of Millie's giggles lifted her mood and Floyd's. 'It's lovely that you want my soul, although it does make you sound like some kind of monster. It is worth so much more than someone just wanting my body. There is something nice about someone thinking you're sexy though. It's thrilling to undress someone and see they're turned on by you, isn't it?' she said.

'I wouldn't know. I've never undressed someone like that,' Floyd replied.

Millie gasped. 'You're a virgin?' she questioned.

'Yeah. I know that's not cool, but it is how it is. I want my first time to be with the woman I love, who I'm going to marry,' Floyd confirmed.

The sparkle in Millie's eyes assured Floyd she wasn't put off by this. It had worried him that, given her past, she'd want someone who was an expert in the bedroom with as much experience as her.

'Oh, that's cute, and *great* news for me. I get to teach you sex! You can learn to do it just the way I like it,' Millie enthused.

'I never imagined a girlfriend taking the news like that. I'm well into my twenties. I thought I'd get laughed at,' Floyd muttered.

'Not at all. You being a virgin is exciting, and it gives me panties-down-time feelings, but it isn't funny. I don't see any reason to laugh at you for saving yourself for The One,' Millie told Floyd.

In the hope it would turn her panties-down-time feelings into kissy-cuddly ones, Millie ordered: 'Kiss me, but kiss me soft.'

As Millie demanded, Floyd brushed his lips against hers for a tantalising second. A moment later, he laid a kiss on her forehead.

With Floyd's lips on her forehead, Millie felt her heart melt. It had done the trick.

A person approached the sign Millie was standing by and loitered by it, gazing out at the traffic on the lookout for public transport, for that was the purpose of the bus stop.

Without a word to each other, Millie and Floyd knew their time at the bus stop had come to an end. They held hands and wandered back towards the shop.

As they walked, Millie saw Floyd's brows furrow. 'What are you thinking?' she asked.

'I was wondering what made you stop sleeping around,' Floyd replied.

Memories of the first time she'd met Cecilia played in Millie's head. She could still recall the words that had changed her life forever.

'I thought I was pregnant. My period was late and some of the sex I'd been having was unprotected. The idea that I could have a baby at nineteen years old got me all scaredy,' Millie revealed.

'Wow,' Floyd murmured.

'I've been tested since then. A few months after the scare, I took myself to a sexual health clinic. They were really lovely there and not at all judgy. The tests they did came back clear, so I somehow managed not to catch anything,' Millie assured Floyd.

'Cool. Thanks for telling me that. I was trying to work out how to ask politely,' Floyd admitted.

By now, Millie and Floyd were back in the supermarket car park. They paused to let a driver get their car out of its space before continuing their conversation and their journey.

'I wouldn't have stopped if Cecilia hadn't said what she'd said. I worked myself up into a frenzy when I realised my period was a week late and called Jude. He flew across to Cambridge with Cecilia in tow. She'd driven him because something was wrong with his car. When he wasn't around, I told her my attitude to life was "Work hard; play hard". Cecilia, a beautiful and powerful woman who I'd only just met, told me that attitude was what had led to my pregnancy scare. That revelation turned my outlook on life upside down. I relaxed a bit about my studies, no longer worked myself to the bone for the best grades all the time, and I took more care of myself. I haven't had sex since that day, and I let myself put the books down if I'm feeling stressy,' Millie told Floyd.

Floyd squeezed Millie's hand. 'Thanks for sharing this. I love you so much more now I know where you've come from and how you've evolved,' he said.

Every time Floyd used the word love, Millie felt her whole body glow a little. It was something she'd never tire of. Sharing her past had eventually felt so easy and natural. It wasn't a subject she'd ever wanted to talk about, but something about Floyd had opened her up.

Loud music erupted from Floyd's pocket. He pulled his phone out and sighed. 'I do need to speak to her. Are you alright to continue shopping? I dumped our trolley just inside the door on the right?' he asked.

'Yes,' Millie confirmed.

Whilst wondering who had called Floyd, Millie returned to the supermarket, feeling far better than she had when she'd left.

24

Chapter Twenty-four

When Millie leant her phone against the stack of textbooks she'd created on the TV stand and it stayed there, she clapped her hands together. One of the books then shifted and the phone slipped.

'I'll just hold you then,' Millie told her phone.

The phone did not respond.

After she'd picked it up, Millie swiped through her apps to find the one she used for videocalls. As she did so, she wandered over to the sofa. By the time she'd sat down, Millie had told the phone to videocall Maddie.

It didn't take Maddie long to answer. 'Hey, gorgeous girl. Good to see your face,' she said.

'Love your hair! That's even better than I imagined!' Millie cried.

Whilst blushing, Maddie ran a hand through her newly-silver locks. 'Thanks. I'd definitely have this colour again,' she replied.

'Very good. And have you shown off your snazzy hair anywhere?' Millie asked.

'Not exactly, but I've been out with it. I drove into Aylesbury to take a look at all the Christmas lights. I feel like part of the decorations a bit now. Silver is very seasonal,' Maddie said.

'Definitely,' Millie agreed.

Maddie gasped. 'Oh, and I popped into this quirky gift shop and saw the best little stocking filler for Mum. It was only a tenner, so I had to get it,' she told Millie.

Forgetting she was on camera, Millie frowned. She tried to ignore that Maddie had far more money than her. The way she dismissively spoke about spending ten pounds on a stocking filler was an unwelcome reminder. In many other ways, Maddie was similar to her.

'*It's churlish to be cross with Maddie for having wealthy parents,*' Millie thought.

A very excited Maddie disappeared from screen for a moment and returned with a little rectangular thing in her hands. Millie worked out it was an orange leather purse with two googly eyes on it. The oddity of it made her smile.

'Mum loves silly things like this. It will make her so happy,' Maddie enthused, lowering herself onto a sofa.

As she had only bought her parents presents that Maddie would think of as stocking fillers, Millie didn't comment.

A bundle of tan and white fur jumped onto Maddie's lap. 'Aw, Trixie wants to meet you!' she said.

The cute dog on screen took away Millie's vexation. She waved at Trixie. 'Hi, Maddie's dog!' Millie replied.

After barking at Millie, Trixie leapt to the floor off screen and padded away in search of treats.

'Anyway, I've talked lots about me, but this call wasn't just for you to admire my hair. Tell me about you. How are things going with heart-meltingly sweet housemate?' Maddie asked.

When she brought to mind her feelings for Floyd, Millie found she couldn't look down the lens. 'I'm smitten. A smitten puppy,' Millie admitted.

Maddie laughed. 'It's smitten *kitten*, but that's fine. I'm so happy that you're smitten, whatever baby animal you are,' she replied.

'Smitten puppy is something my brother says. He has his own Jude Austen versions of expressions,' Millie explained.

'Ah, then your brother is very funny,' Maddie commented.

Millie heard a door being opened. She assumed it was on Maddie's end of the line, so thought nothing of it. She wasn't expecting Floyd back for a while.

'I'm really looking forward to celebrating with Jude and the family, but I'll miss Floyd terribly. I go tomorrow, and I don't know how I'll cope, not coming down to find him in the kitchen each morning. I'll miss him so...' Millie began. She tailed off when the subject of her speech entered the room.

'I'm guessing he's just walked in,' Maddie said.

Millie looked from Floyd to the clock on the wall behind him and realised she'd previously misread the time. When Floyd smiled at her and waved, she returned the gesture.

'Well, Miss Smitten Puppy, I don't want to keep you from your beau. If I can have a look at him, I'll say goodbye and let you go,' Maddie told Millie.

When Millie nodded her approval, Floyd sat next to her and leant to be in shot. He waved at the camera and said: 'You must be Maddie. I've heard a lot about you.'

Maddie leant towards her screen and stared intently for a good few seconds. When she sat back, there was a smile on her face. 'You'll do,' she commented.

'Glad I'm M and M approved,' Floyd replied.

'If you make our gorgeous girl happy, that's all that matters. From what I've heard, you make her *very* happy,' Maddie told Floyd.

Both Floyd and Millie blushed. Neither of them knew how to answer.

'Anyway, like I said, I'll let you go. Merry Christmas, Millie,' Maddie said.

'Merry Christmas,' Millie and Floyd replied in unison.

Here endeth the videocall.

25

Chapter Twenty-five

The little suitcase on her bed stirred mixed emotions in Millie when she looked upon it. The heartache of leaving Floyd competed with the excitement of knowing she was going to see her family.

Once she'd packed her emotions deep inside herself and some clothes and presents in her suitcase, Millie headed downstairs. Floyd was in the kitchen. She could smell that he was making her toast. As she thought he was nearly done, Millie waited in the lounge.

When Floyd appeared with toast and handed a plate to her, Millie commented: 'Just how I like it.'

'Well, it's the last time I get to make it for you for a couple of days, so I was determined to get it right,' Floyd replied.

Though she'd thought she had it under control, sadness welled up inside Millie. 'Don't say that! I can't think about the fact I have to be parted from you,' she whined.

The smile Floyd gave her settled Millie a little. 'It's only for a few days. Then we'll be together for the rest of the year,' he pointed out.

'But what about the new year? I have to go back to Cambridge.

Then I'll be even further from you. Can our relationship survive long-distance?' Millie replied.

'No need to think about that now. Eat your perfect toast before it gets cold,' Floyd swiftly replied.

The brusque response was out of character for Floyd. Millie was taken aback. Whilst chewing a mouthful of toast, as ordered, she realised it was probably a sign he was just as upset as her that they were about to part.

~

Thanks to his kind boss, Floyd had a half day at work. This meant he was able to stand with Millie as she gazed out of the front room window waiting for Jude's Suzuki Swift to appear.

When he looked at Millie, holding her suitcase and not taking her eyes off the road outside, Floyd was overwhelmed with love. He wrapped her up in an impromptu hug. 'I'll miss you,' Floyd whispered.

The warmth of Floyd's body against hers and the tickle of his breath against her ear gave Millie tingles. She maintained the connection between them by hugging him back, keeping him close for as long as she could.

After the hug had ended, Millie opened her mouth to tell Floyd she'd miss him too. She closed it again when she decided their loving embrace had communicated the same message.

'I can't wait to see Jude and tell him how fabulous living with you is,' Millie said.

Dread clutched at Floyd's heart. 'You won't tell him about us, will you? The nature of our relationship, I mean?' he asked.

Millie sighed. 'No, I won't. You're being a silly-Floydy though. As I've said before, he isn't the type to punch your lights out because you're in love with his sister. When he finds out, which won't be because I told him, he'll be thrilled,' she replied.

The insult "silly-Floydy" was far too cute for Floyd to take offense to it. He almost wanted to irritate Millie more so she'd call him it again. '*This bodes well if, when we argue, all I can think about is how adorable she is. This girl really is The One,*' Floyd thought.

Just as Floyd was wondering what to talk to Millie about to distract them from the fact that she was about to leave, Jude pulled up outside. Millie's chariot awaited.

26

Chapter Twenty-six

For the drive from Floyd's house to his family home, Jude played his favourite Christmas songs. Though they didn't speak to each other much, he and Millie belted out *I Wish It Could Be Christmas Everyday*.

When they reached the four-bed semi on the edge of Colchester they'd grown up in, Jude said to his sister: 'Welcome home.'

Waiting at the door for their children's homecoming were Sue and Alan Austen. As soon as the Suzuki Swift that had just pulled into the drive was stationary, Millie jumped out and ran into Sue's arms. She remained snuggled into her mother's chest whilst her brother got her suitcase out the boot, because that was where Floyd had put it, and carried it towards the house.

'Was the drive from the station okay?' Alan asked.

Until that moment, Jude had forgotten his parents were under the impression Millie had spent most of December in Cambridge, and had just come by train from there. It only took him a second to get it into his head so he could reply: 'Yeah, fine.'

'We karaoked in the car to Christmas songs,' Millie told her parents.

Both Millie's parents smiled at her. 'Lovely, dearest,' they said in unison.

'Have you put Millie up in her old room?' Jude asked.

'Yeah, she's in her own room. You can have your room if you like, but I thought Brandon's might be better. He's got a double, which you'll need when Cecilia gets here tomorrow. Brandon refuses to stay over, so you may as well use it,' Alan replied.

'Cool. I'll take this up to Millie's room. Might spend the night in there myself if she fancies a sibling sleepover,' Jude said.

Millie gasped. 'Oh, please do that! I miss our sibling sleepovers,' she begged.

The enthusiasm in his sister's voice gave Jude a spring in his step as he took her suitcase upstairs.

With nothing she had to do, Millie followed her parents into the lounge. The fibre-optic tree she'd grown up with dominated one corner of the room with its six feet of colour-changing branches. Underneath it were presents wrapped in shiny silver paper. They were all square, which told her nothing about the contents. Her parents put all gifts in boxes, no matter how small the present was, before wrapping them, to make it harder to guess what was inside.

The air in the lounge was heavy with the scent of satsumas. Millie inhaled deeply and sighed.

'Ah, yeah, I got some baby orange things. You have to at Christmas,' Alan told Millie, nodding at a fruit bowl full of satsumas on the coffee table.

'Yummy. I love them. So Christmassy,' Millie replied.

'You can have some after dinner. It's just cheese and ham sandwiches,' Sue said.

The mention of food caught Jude's attention as he entered the room. 'Ah, simple tea. That's good with me,' Jude commented.

A rumble of Sue's tummy made her son, daughter, and husband stare at her. 'Well excuse me! Seems like I'd best start on those sandwiches now,' she cried.

'I'll help,' Jude replied, following his mum out to the kitchen.

After sharing a look, Millie and her dad also made their way to the kitchen. Making sandwiches was a family affair.

-

As Jude was a fast eater, he finished his sandwiches quicker than the rest of his family. This meant his hands were free to pick up his phone and look at the photo Cecilia had sent him. The pixels on his screen made up a picture of fun and friendship. Cecilia's blue eyes were shining as she stood next to Tamsyn and Emma-Leigh.

To his wife-to-be, Jude wrote: "Have a great time."

'Have you just got a message from Cecilia by any chance?' Sue asked.

'Yeah. How'd you know?' Jude questioned.

'Your face lit up. It had to be her,' Sue explained.

Though he'd been perfectly able to reply to Cecilia, Jude couldn't find the words to answer his mum. His cheeks reddened, but that was the only response he gave.

'Aw, my boy's in love!' Sue cried.

'Yeah, I am. I'm head over toes in love with Cecilia,' Jude admitted.

Both Jude's parents smiled at him. 'Lovely, dearest,' they said in unison.

To get away from people talking about how loved up he was, Jude took his plate over to the laminate kitchen worktop.

'Is there anyone in your life, Millie, who makes you all red-cheeked and tongue-tied when he messages you? You must have met some nice boys at uni,' Sue asked.

With Floyd's wishes on her mind, Millie replied: 'There's no romance on the horizon that I can tell you about.'

It saddened Millie to see her mum's smile turn upside down. If only she could tell her about Floyd.

It wasn't just Millie who saw Sue frown. Her husband did too. Alan didn't share his wife's unconcealed disappointment at their daughter's single status. To make his views known, he told Millie: 'That's as fine as one of those autumn days when you don't actually need a jumper. We don't need our kids to be all loved up. We just want them happy, whatever that looks like.'

~

Before settling with Millie for the night, Jude slipped into his pyjamas in what had been Brandon's room. He entered Millie's room to find her pumping up an air mattress.

'Here we are. It's all full of air and plumpfy now, ready for you to sleep on,' Millie told her brother, gesturing at the air mattress on the floor as if it was a prize in a gameshow.

'Thanks for that,' Jude replied.

When Millie jumped into bed, Jude gingerly lowered himself onto his. The air mattress hardly budged under his weight. He fidgeted a little before concluding that it didn't make a difference what position he laid in.

'My bed is higher, so I am superior to you,' Millie commented.

'Yes, Queen Millie,' Jude agreed.

Taking on an affected tone, Millie ordered: 'Prove you are a loyal subject by kissing my feet.'

'At once, Queen Millie' Jude replied.

The duvet Jude had just pulled over himself was thrown on the floor as he got up and made his way to the bottom of Millie's bed. Unlike his own, Jude took great care with Millie's duvet. He gently pealed back the bottom corner to reveal her feet and then lowered his lips to her toes. His retreat was much swifter as Millie squirmed, almost kicking him in the face.

'Ew, that's disgusting! I didn't actually expect you to kiss my tootsies!' Millie cried.

Jude shrugged. 'Just doing as I'm told,' he pointed out.

When Millie and Jude's eyes met, they burst out laughing. They both felt at least a decade younger.

The laughter in Millie's room was so loud that it could be heard in the next room, where their parents were. 'That sound is the best Christmas present I could wish for,' Sue whispered.

As he agreed with his wife, Alan kissed the woman who'd given him the laughing children.

27

Chapter Twenty-seven

'I could stay here in your arms all day. I don't want presents, dry poultry, or a visit from Santa. You're all I want. *This* is all I want. I don't even want sleep. I don't care that it's excessively early in the morning. You're here,' Cecilia murmured.

When Cecilia spoke, Jude felt her breath on his shoulder. It gave him a little thrill. He hugged her closer and whispered back: 'Me too, but that's what we did last year.'

Cecilia sighed. The exhalation of air simultaneously expressed contentment and frustration. 'And it was *blissful*. I love my future in-laws and enjoyed spending time with them yesterday, even if I was hungover, but I love you more. Once I'm up, it'll be fine. I feel like one of the family already, which is most wonderful. Right now though, it's hard to imagine anything better than this warm bed and your naked body against mine,' she said.

To let her know he felt the same, Jude kissed Cecilia. Her mouth moaned against his, which inspired him to deepen the kiss. Together they made the moment last as long as possible.

After ending the kiss to breathe, Jude told Cecilia: 'That was my first Christmas present to you.'

'May I return it?' Cecilia asked.

Jude chuckled softly. 'Usually that would be an insult, but in this case...' he began.

Due to Cecilia kissing him, Jude never got to finish his sentence. After a second of his lips being locked with hers, he couldn't remember what he was going to tell her.

Their second Christmas Day kiss ended abruptly when Jude and Cecilia heard shouting and banging on the landing. They disentangled from each other and sat bolt upright.

There was then knocking on Jude and Cecilia's bedroom door. 'It's Christmas!' Millie yelled through the closed door.

Jude groaned. 'And that's why Brandon is in a hotel,' he said.

The sound of Millie gigging with pure glee outside their door made her brother and future sister-in-law laugh with her.

~

As they'd been disturbed, Jude and Cecilia thought it was best to just get up and go downstairs. So did Alan and Sue.

It was Jude and Cecilia who were the first couple to enter the lounge. They found Millie sitting on the sofa sporting a Christmas jumper with a tree on it. When Millie saw she had company, she reached inside the jumper and flicked a switch. The knitted tree on her jumper now had real twinkling fairy lights on it.

'That is most cheery,' Cecilia commented.

'Of course. It's Christmas,' Millie replied.

'Ain't that the one Brandon bought you?' Jude questioned.

'Yes, and he'll be here in an hour, as long as his taxi is on time,' Millie confirmed.

Cheerier than the Christmas jumper, in Cecilia's opinion, were the smiles exchanged by Millie and Jude. The Austen family were tight-knit and very loving, yet willing to accept her as part of them.

Behind Cecilia, Alan and Sue walked in. They said: 'Merry Christmas, guys.'

Rousing cries of "Merry Christmas" filled the little room.

'Shall we head into the kitchen? I'll get the dinner on whilst you put together our traditional Christmas breakfast, Jude,' Sue suggested.

Jude nodded, and that was all the encouragement Sue needed. She led her family into the room with laminate worktops and oak dining table with the leaves up and six chairs around it, two of which didn't match the table. A shiny silver American-style fridge-freezer towered over Sue at one end of the worktop.

'What is your traditional Christmas breakfast?' Cecilia hissed to Jude.

'Awesome. That's what it is,' Jude whispered back.

After Sue had removed a whole turkey from it, Jude took a netted bag of little round cheeses wrapped in bright red wax from the fridge. Millie was busy opening and closing cupboards. She eventually pulled a selection box of crackers down from a wall cupboard. Alan danced around his family to get to the plates, which were kept in the cupboard next to the oven. He placed five plain white ones on the surface.

Watching the Austen family work as a well-oiled machine made Cecilia feel left out. She withdrew physically and mentally, retreating to the back of the room.

When Jude returned to the fridge-freezer for cheese of a different variety, he read his fiancée's expression, which gave him a glimpse into her mind. 'Cecilia, could you unwrap the baby cheeses? They're well fiddly,' he requested.

A smile lit up Cecilia's face. 'Of course,' she agreed.

As he passed the bag to her, Jude told Cecilia: 'Two for each of us, cos we've also got a big block of Red Lancaster that Dad's cutting up. I'll bring a plate to put the naked cheeses on.'

After making sure she'd turned the dial on the oven to the correct temperature, Sue glanced over at the dining table. She watched Cecilia unwrapping cheeses and placing the wax on the sea of plastic outer wrappers she'd laid on the table. This year the wax would not be turned into an abstract model that left a mark on the table. That was an unexpected but very welcome Christmas present for Sue.

-

A knock on the door made Millie squeal with excitement. 'Brandon's here!' she cried.

No-one stopped Millie when she jumped up and dashed to the front door. The last time she'd seen her oldest brother was last Christmas. It had been a whole year since all three Austen siblings had shared a room.

Just as Millie had hoped, Brandon was standing outside in the cold when she opened the door. Before he could say a word, she stepped out to be with him and wrapped him in her tightest hug. 'You're home,' she said to his chest.

'Merry Christmas, baby sister,' Brandon replied.

The hug was abruptly ended by Millie so she could stare up at him. 'I'm not a baby. I'm in my twenties now,' she protested.

'And I turned thirty-one this year, so you'll always be my baby sister,' Brandon told Millie.

After giggling, Millie pulled Brandon in for another cuddle. 'And I will always love you, even though you're old,' she said.

'You're letting the heat out!' Alan yelled from the kitchen.

Their father shouting prompted Brandon and Millie to head indoors. As it had once been his home, Brandon knew where the kitchen was, and he knew that's where he'd find the rest of the family.

The second he saw him, Alan jumped up from the dining table and made a beeline for Brandon. He gave him a slap on the back. 'Merry Christmas, son,' he said.

Over his dad's shoulder, Brandon spotted the only person in the room he hadn't met. Her long blonde hair and serene smile stunned him. He couldn't believe the woman he was looking at was his little brother's fiancée.

'*You're* Cecilia?' Brandon questioned, looking at the woman next to Jude.

Cecilia nodded. 'I am. Nice to meet you. I've heard a lot about you,' she confirmed.

When Jude caught the look in his brother's eye, he grinned. 'Yeah, she's a stunner, and she's just as lovely on the inside. I'm a very lucky man,' he commented.

Looking at Cecilia, Brandon couldn't picture her married to Jude. He certainly couldn't work out why someone like her wanted to be with his brother.

'It's so good to see you, my boy. Are you ready to head off to church?' Sue asked.

'You too, Mum, and yes, I am. I knew we'd be heading out pretty sharpish,' Brandon replied.

'Would you mind awfully if I don't come? I do not feel comfortable in churches, and I like to have a quiet moment to myself at Christmas. May I remain here?' Cecilia requested.

Alan shrugged. 'Yeah, of course. Do what you wanna do. We ain't massively religious. It's just something we do on His birthday. While we're out is the only quiet time you're gonna get. We Austens are pretty loud,' he told Cecilia.

With that decided, the Austens headed to the hall to get their coats, except Millie, who lingered in the kitchen with Cecilia.

'Are you okay?' Cecilia asked.

'That's what I was going to ask *you*. You sounded sad when you said you needed a quiet moment,' Millie replied.

'Oh, that. Yes, I'm fine, thank you. I just need to take a minute on special occasions to think about Mum,' Cecilia explained.

From the hall, a voice called for Millie. She looked from Cecilia to the door and back again.

'Go. I'll be fine,' Cecilia assured Millie.

Once again, someone shouted Millie's name. It was clear she had to go. Before leaving her, Millie pulled Cecilia in for a hug. She held her future sister-in-law tight, as if trying to squeeze the sadness out of her.

When Jude popped his head round the door, Millie left his fiancée and joined him in the hallway.

'Poor girl. Family *is* Christmas for us. I can't imagine Mum and Dad not being here,' Millie murmured.

With a sad smile on his face, Jude replied: 'Family are more precious than anything you can put under the tree.'

28

Chapter Twenty-eight

Mouth-watering scents drifted across the kitchen. They were accompanied by chatter from the table.

As he was neither cooking nor talking, Brandon wasn't contributing to the sights and sounds of the room. He was watching Cecilia plate things up alongside Alan. They'd been cooking together for the best part of an hour, dodging round each other to complete their various tasks, and had barely exchanged a dozen words.

Unlike his fiancée, Jude had spoken many words in the last hour, most of them to his sister.

'What did one Christmas light say to the other Christmas light?' Jude asked Millie, holding a tiny strip of paper.

'Oh, Oh! I know! Hang around with me and your life will be brighter!' Millie cried.

Jude's laughter echoed around the room.

'Isn't that the wrong way round? You're the one reading the joke. Why are you also the one laughing?' Brandon questioned.

'Her answer is a lot better than the one on the paper,' Jude replied.

'What do you mean it is better than the answer on paper? My answer is the right one!' Millie protested.

'Uh-uh, no it's not. It says here: "You light me up",' Jude told his sister.

With a frown on her face and a paper crown on her head, Millie snatched the joke from Jude's hand. She then picked up the tiny pencil she'd acquired earlier that day and scribbled furiously on her recently-stolen piece of paper. Once she was finished with it, she shoved it over to Jude.

When he picked it up, Jude saw Millie had crossed out the original punchline to the joke and jotted down her own response.

'There. Now it is correct. No more Christmas crackers. I do not wish to correct any more erroneous jokes,' Millie said.

'And good timing too. Dinner is served,' Cecilia replied as she placed a very full plate in front of Jude.

'You're supposed to serve me first,' Millie pointed out.

Cecilia, who had been heading over to the worktop to get the next plate, froze. All the confidence she'd built in the last few hours abandoned her. 'Sorry,' she murmured.

'Oh, it's cool. Millie being served first at Christmas is a family joke. One year, when she were little, she snuck downstairs before any of us was up and opened all her presents. Dad told her off and said she weren't getting any Christmas dinner. When dinner time came, he served one by one, leaving her last, or at least that was the plan. Halfway through she started crying. She really thought she wasn't getting Christmas dinner. Every year since then, she's been served first, to assure her that she's actually getting food. It's cool, Cecilia. You've done nothing wrong,' Jude rapidly explained.

The tension that had been building in Cecilia since Millie had piped up was released in the form of a sigh. 'Thanks, Jude,' she said.

Now able to carry on, Cecilia brought two more plates over, one of them Millie's. Alan plonked a gravy boat down in the middle of the table. With their work done, the pair took their seats and tucked in.

After taking his first mouthful of carrots, Brandon noticed there were no discs of the sweet orange vegetable on Jude's plate. In that moment, Brandon wished he had someone who could know he was stressed without a word and calm him in an instant, or someone who knew what veg he hated and remembered not to put it on his plate. Those unspoken gestures were, to him, love.

-

'What a lovely speech! He really captured the spirit of Christmas and this country!' Sue commented.

'Long live the king!' Alan cried.

Though she'd enjoyed the speech, Millie had been slightly distracted by the things wrapped in shiny paper bearing tags with her name on under the tree.

'I suppose it's present time then,' Alan said, grinning at Millie.

The moment she heard the word "presents", Millie jumped off the sofa and dashed over to the tree. She picked up the four things she'd spent most of King Charles's speech thinking about and brought them over to the sofa, handing one to everyone except her dad.

'Aw, are these from you?' Sue asked.

'Yes. A lovely lady took me Christmas shopping. Please, please open them! I can't wait!' Millie begged.

As requested, Millie's loved ones opened their gifts from her. Her parents worked together to unwrap their gift, smiling when they revealed the ribbons under the paper.

'Oh, you got me sweets? I love sweets! Cheers, Millie!' Jude said.

'I promise not to snaffle these sweeties. They're tongue-tingly ones, so I wouldn't want them anyway,' Millie replied.

Alan was running a ribbon chain through his fingers. 'How cool.

Like a paper chain, but you can use it year after year,' he realised out loud.

'That's the idea. A local crafty lady made it,' Millie confirmed.

'This chocolate is not going to last anywhere near as long as that ribbon chain. It definitely won't be around next Christmas,' Brandon commented.

'Nor these violet creams. They are my favourites. I'm most pleased,' Cecilia added.

Happy that her gifts had been well received, Millie asked: 'Do I get prezzies now?'

~

Across town from Millie, Floyd was also opening a present from her. He tore open the paper, sending the glitter that had been attached to it all over the lounge, to reveal a purple book. He stroked his fingers over the title, *A Christmas Celebration*. As he often did when he picked up a new book, Floyd began to flick through the pages. He paused immediately when he found Millie's writing on the title page. It read: "I hope this story is as romantic as the one we've created in real life, Millie".

In the absence of the woman who'd given him such a beautiful gift, Floyd hugged the book. He imagined her skipping on the way home from town, delighted to have bought something so wonderful. The only thing he'd have liked more than the book with her words inside was Millie herself.

Whilst daydreaming about Millie, Floyd lost track of time. He jumped when his phone buzzed to inform him of a videocall. When he answered it, his mum asked: 'Why are you crying?'

It was news to Floyd that there were tears rolling down his cheeks. 'I'm fine. I just opened a present from a woman I love,' he assured his mum.

'The socks weren't that good,' Floyd's mum said.

Floyd chuckled. Deciding not to correct his mum, he told her: 'It's the thought that counts.'

29

Chapter Twenty-nine

After the longest hug either of them had ever had, Floyd led Millie into their lounge. She left her suitcase in the hallway. It didn't matter as much as being with Floyd did.

'Would you like your Christmas present from me?' Floyd asked.

'What sort of a question is that? Who would say no?' Millie replied.

'It's good to have you back,' Floyd commented with a grin.

'It'd be even better if I had my prezzie,' Millie pointed out.

Chuckling as he did so, Floyd made his way to the TV unit, opened the small drawer that Millie had always assumed was empty, and pulled out a slim present wrapped in bright red paper and adorned with a silver ribbon tied up in a bow. Then, he handed it to Millie.

Instead of opening it, Millie gazed at it in wonder. She'd never seen such a pretty present.

'I adored my present from you. It was so sweet! I've heard of Heidi Swain before, but haven't come across her in the charity shops, and you know I don't buy books new. What you wrote inside was beautiful,' Floyd told Millie.

Hugging her present to her chest, Millie flopped onto the sofa. 'A lady in the bookshop helped me choose it. I told her what I'd seen on your shelf, and that's what she recommended,' she explained.

'How nice of you to think to do that, and impressive that you took note of what was on my shelf,' Floyd said.

In response, Millie just shrugged.

With Floyd watching, Millie untied the ribbon around her present and pulled it off. She then wrapped it round her neck like a scarf. Now wearing a ribbon, she gently undid the sticky tape holding the present closed. When she opened up the paper, Millie found a large notebook inside. The cover was hot pink and had stickers on that spelt out: "Millie and Floyd's Dream Dates."

'What is it?' Millie asked.

'Originally, it was a point journal. It is now a place to jot down dating ideas for our future,' Floyd explained.

The word future stood out to Millie. Floyd's behaviour had led her to believe, certainly to hope, what they had was more than a holiday romance. It had occurred to her though that he hadn't mentioned her return to Cambridge in the new year. Clearly, he did have plans for them, unless he thought they were going to have a very busy last week together. This gave Millie a buzz of excitement.

'It's personal! How sweet. Thank you,' Millie said.

'I've seen these "couple's goals" and "shared bucket list" premade journals for sale online, and they inspired me to make our own one,' Floyd revealed.

To show how much she loved it, Millie kissed the homemade journal of dream dates. The rubbery cover felt funny under her lips, but this didn't stop her kissing it three more times.

'I'm jealous of my present,' Floyd told Millie.

The journal Floyd was jealous of was thrown on the sofa. Millie then jumped up and kissed him. It was a forceful smack on the lips which elicited no romantic feelings within him.

'Happy now?' Millie questioned.

'Yeah, sure,' Floyd replied with a grin.

When Floyd sat next to Millie, her eye was drawn to his wrist. There was a watch on it. She'd never noticed it before.

'I got one of those fitness watches for Christmas from my parents, and also some socks. It checks my heart rate, counts my steps, stuff like that. The watch, not my socks. You can have weekly challenges with friends to see who gets the most steps, and Mum's added me to our family one. I'm bottom, of course,' Floyd told Millie.

A thought popped into Floyd's head. 'Do you fancy a walk?' he asked.

'Yes, I've spent lots of time surrounded by walls over the last few days. A walk would be great, as long as I can have a cuppa to warm me up when I get back,' Millie replied.

Another thought popped into Floyd's head. This one he kept to himself.

-

For the entire walk from the house she shared with him to Castle Park, Millie wondered what was in Floyd's bag. She'd nipped upstairs to unpack her suitcase and found Floyd wearing a little blue rucksack on her return. Previous experience taught her not to enquire about its contents. She knew Floyd liked to surprise her, and he knew she enjoyed it.

'I'd like to find a nice bench to sit on for a moment,' Floyd said.

A few steps down the path from where Floyd had announced his intentions of sitting for a moment was a black metal bench overlooking the boating lake. Millie had always thought of it as the bird lake, for avian life often seemed to congregate there, usually seagulls. On that chilly December day, there were no boats or birds on the lake. The only signs of any life around the pond were Millie and Floyd themselves, who made their way to the bench.

Before sitting down, Floyd removed his back pack. He opened it up and pulled out a flask and a packet of marshmallows.

Millie gasped. 'Hot chocolate?' she asked.

'Yeah. I hope you like it,' Floyd confirmed.

'Of course! It's hot chocolate. Who wouldn't like it, except perhaps people who are allergic to chocolate or hotness?' Millie replied.

'I'm certainly not allergic to hotness. If I was, I couldn't be around you,' Floyd said.

'Smooth. Very smooth. Not very you though,' Millie pointed out

The flask had two plastic cups on top. Floyd handed one to Millie, who held it for him to pour hot chocolate into. Once he'd poured himself a cup too and set it to one side on the bench, he closed the flask and opened the packet of marshmallows. He dropped a couple of the soft and small white sweets into Millie's cup.

'So pretty. Why would anyone buy a hot chocolate from somewhere like Starbucks for silly money when you can make something as lovely as this?' Millie wondered aloud.

'I'm so pleased you said that. I thought you might think I didn't care about you because I didn't get you one of those expensive drinks from a cafe,' Floyd revealed.

'Making it yourself shows you care about me far more than just getting a fancy-pantsy hot chocolate from a chain would have. You've made this romantic,' Millie said.

'Everything is romantic with you. Your presence makes things special,' Floyd replied.

To be sure she'd heard them right, Millie replayed Floyd's words in her head. Once she'd confirmed she had, warmth spread from her heart throughout her body. Her cheeks turned red and her lips curved up.

When Floyd put an arm around her, Millie scooted across the

bench to get as close to him as possible. They sat in shared silence, staring out at the still water of the boating lake.

As she was right next to him, Millie saw Floyd's new watch light up. A message rolled across the screen that said: "application successful." Like Millie, Floyd saw the words on his watch. Neither of them read the conclusion of the message, as he turned his wrist upside down.

'Oh, that was just a work thing. A boring work thing,' Floyd hastily told Millie.

Something in Floyd's tone suggested to Millie there was more to the message than he was letting on. As he clearly didn't want to talk about it, she didn't ask about it. She didn't ask about anything. All the couple did was sit together, enjoying post-Christmas calm. They were both content.

30

Chapter Thirty

A quick mental count told Floyd, on average, six out of ten dissatisfied customers he'd spoken to that day had left the mobile network he worked for. It was a poor performance compared to his usual stats. They'd all cited splurging at Christmas and a need to cut back on costs as reasons to leave Floyd's employer. The network he worked for was good, but not cheap. As he told his customers: 'A Volkswagen is cheaper than a Ferrari. You get what you pay for.' Much to Floyd's dismay, one of the people he'd had to speak to that day replied: 'But I don't need a Ferrari. A VW suits my needs fine.'

The supervisor was walking round the office, peering over peoples' shoulders to read their computer screens. She strode down the aisles of desks with silent footsteps. When she reached Floyd, she paused and leant over him.

'Did I hear you got a message from HR yesterday?' the supervisor hissed into Floyd's ear.

'Yeah,' Floyd confirmed.

The supervisor tutted. 'The news shocked and saddened me,' she said.

'Sorry, but you contributed to this,' Floyd pointed out.

'And now I seriously regret that. You're due a break. Tell the computer you're away and come find me by that stupid triangular planter outside,' the supervisor ordered.

As she had nothing more to say, the supervisor left her workers unsupervised and headed downstairs.

Once he'd selected the staff meeting option on his work computer, Floyd stood and made his way out of the room. Before descending the metal staircase to meet his boss, he pulled his phone out. In his haste, Floyd opened his contacts app instead of the texting one. Whilst cursing himself in his head, he scrolled through the list it brought up until he got to "Austen" and chose the first option. To that person he wrote: "This is a LONG day. Can't wait to get home to you, Millie. Just thinking of it gives me kissy-cuddly feelings, as you so cutely put it. All my love, Floyd xxx XXX xxx." Without pausing to check it, Floyd sent the text. He then descended the stairs to deal with his supervisor.

-

Texting the first Austen in his contacts gave Floyd a boost. He managed to convince every customer he spoke to from that moment on to stay with his employer. In some cases, he had to cajole them with promises of discounts or gift cards, but it worked.

When a colleague returned from a cigarette break midway through the afternoon, it occurred to Floyd, although he wasn't addicted to nicotine, he could take a moment for himself. He decided to use that moment to check if Millie had answered his text. The absence of a notification from his SMS app told Floyd she hadn't replied.

Footsteps from his supervisor prompted Floyd to return his phone to his pocket.

'Relax, Floyd. You spend more than enough time helping other people with their phones. I don't care if you glance at Insta or whatever every now and again. As long as you're not searching for tractors at work, I'm happy,' the supervisor said.

The reference to bad behaviour in parliament made Floyd snicker. 'Cheers, but I should work. I just wanted to check that someone hadn't text me,' he replied.

This satisfied the supervisor. She nodded and walked on.

Though he wasn't satisfied, as Millie hadn't answered him, Floyd also continued with his work.

~

As soon as Millie heard the door open, she jumped up to greet Floyd. They met in the doorway to the lounge, where they kissed under the fake mistletoe.

'I feel dirty. Is it okay if I grab a shower?' Floyd asked when his lips were free from kissing.

'It's horrid to feel all grimy. Yes, grab a shower. You can even turn it on and get clean under the water if you want,' Millie replied.

Whilst chuckling, Floyd skipped up the stairs. Millie watched him go, letting his laugher play on repeat in her head.

Once Floyd was out of sight, Millie trudged back to the lounge. Her textbook was still open on the sofa with two notebooks beside it. She plonked herself down next to them and read up to a good stopping point, making a note in one of her notebooks so she couldn't lose her place in the book.

Just as Millie was wondering what to do with herself until Floyd got downstairs from his shower, there was a knock at the door. When she opened it, her heart soared. Jude was standing there.

'Hello! What are you doing here? We'll be seeing you in a few days for New Year's,' Millie questioned.

'I got a question for you. Do you love Floyd, like *love* him?' Jude asked.

A stunned Millie blurted out: 'Yes, I adore him, and the feeling is mutual, but how do you know that?'

When his sister confirmed she adored Floyd, Jude grinned. 'Never mind how I know. All I'll tell you is that I'm really happy for you two. Now, where is he?' he replied.

'Upstairs, in the shower,' Millie revealed.

'Good. Please stand in the hallway and look shocked, maybe gasp a few times. When the time seems right, put a hand on my shoulder and beg me to calm down,' Jude said.

'What?' Millie questioned.

'Please just play along and let me have a bit of fun,' Jude begged.

Now curious, Millie nodded her consent to Jude's plan.

Having been given permission, Jude stepped inside and slammed the door. He then stormed over to the foot of the stairs.

This fearsome behaviour told Millie what Jude was going to do. She snickered but stifled the laughter when Jude glared at her.

'Floyd! Get your arse down here right now!' Jude yelled.

There was no response from upstairs.

After banging his fist on the wall, Jude shouted: 'Mr Floyd Kiernan! Don't make me come up there!'

That was all Jude could shout, as a coughing fit overcame him. When that was over, he stared at his hand and rubbed the side of it with his other thumb. 'Being an alpha male, protective big brother, tough guy hurts,' he commented.

Jude was saved further pain, as Floyd made an appearance sporting a fluffy pink towel round his waist. The two men, one at the top of the stairs, one at the bottom, stared at each other. Though the standoff amused her, as did the sight of Floyd with her towel wrapped round him, Millie managed to remain silent.

'What the hell is going on?' Floyd asked as he descended the stairs.

'I'll tell you what's going on!' Jude snapped back.

Instead of telling Floyd what was going on, Jude got his phone out and thrust it in Floyd's face. Under messages confirming Jude would bring Cecilia over for dinner a couple of days before Millie left was a text that read: "This is a LONG day. Can't wait to get home to you, Millie. Just thinking of it gives me kissy-cuddly feelings, as you so cutely put it. All my love, Floyd xxx XXX xxx."

'Oh,' Floyd whispered when he realised Jude and Millie both had the surname Austen and J comes before M in the alphabet.

'My mate and my little sis,' Jude said.

'Sorry,' Floyd murmured.

'My mate and my little sister?' Jude questioned.

'Yes,' Floyd confirmed.

Whilst his sister and former housemate watched on with bated breath, Jude inhaled deeply, then exhaled. He repeated this a few times.

'My mate, my mate yeah? The bloke I used to live with, have known for years? You're going out with my little sister?' Jude asked. His nostrils were flared and he continued to breath deeply.

This was the moment Millie had been waiting for. She placed her hand on Jude's shoulder and said: 'Please calm down. I love this man.'

The siblings shared a grin before Jude pulled Floyd into a hug and slapped him on the back. Only then did Floyd realise Jude, and quite possibly Millie, had been playing a game.

'I were just joshing with you. This is brilliant! Well done, mate,' Jude told Floyd.

Now he knew Jude was in fact pleased he was in love with Millie, Floyd returned his hug.

'I said you were being a silly-Floydy and that Jude would be fine about us,' Millie said.

'Yes, dear,' Floyd replied with a smile.

'Charming(!) Well, if that's how you're going to talk to me, I'm going to storm off and make tea,' Millie declared.

With her brother and boyfriend laughing behind her, Millie marched out of the hallway.

Once he was sure Millie was out of earshot, Jude leant in towards Floyd and whispered: 'Do you really think she's the one?'

'Certainly,' Floyd confirmed.

31

Chapter Thirty-one

For their walk to Jude and Cecilia's, Millie and Floyd held hands. They admired plenty of Christmas lights along the way, for it was quite a journey.

When Millie reached her destination and saw the smiles on their hosts faces, she knew it had all been worth it. The warmth of Jude and Cecilia and their home banished the cold that had seeped into Millie's bones.

Delicious scents greeted Millie when she entered the kitchen. Food being cooked for her added to the welcoming atmosphere of the place.

'Dinner is nearly ready. I've got prosecco and beer in the fridge, and vodka and cola in a cupboard. There are also plenty of teabags,' Cecilia told her guests.

'Thanks, splendid hostess. I'll have tea,' Millie replied.

Half of the table was against a wall. Floyd went round to the opposite side and pulled a chair out.

'I don't want to sit looking at the wall. I want to gaze out at the kitchen,' Millie told Floyd.

'But I can't push your chair in on that side,' Floyd pointed out.

'I don't need you to. I can open doors, walk by roads, and pull my chair in. It's fun when you do your daft gentlemanly things, but not *all* the time,' Millie said.

To put an end to the argument, Millie plonked herself down with her back against the wall.

Floyd sat opposite Millie on the chair he'd intended her to sit on.

Whilst Jude made a cup of tea, Cecilia checked on her food. She stuck a meat thermometer into the chicken through one of the gaps in the lattice of golden pastry that covered it. The thermometer confirmed the chicken had reached 75 degrees Celsius, so she was confident it was cooked.

A crackling sound filled the room as Cecilia put a knife through the pastry layer of her chicken en croûte. She sliced all the way through it and did so again a couple more times.

Full of pride, Cecilia brought plates of food she was sure was delicious over to the table. Her fiancé was pouring a splash of vodka into a glass of cola behind her, which he handed to Floyd. As their hosting duties were complete for the time being, Jude and Cecilia joined their guests.

To stop herself burning her mouth by immediately eating the scrummy food in front of her, Millie gazed around the room in search of something to chat about. Her attention settled on Cecilia's t-shirt. 'So, do you like The Script?' Millie asked.

As she knew the comment was prompted by her top, Cecilia looked down at herself. 'Very much. Jude took me to a concert of theirs in Edinburgh. He bought me this as a souvenir,' she explained.

'That sounds lovely,' Millie commented.

'The castle was behind the stage, cos it were an outdoor thing.

They played a really mushy song and Cecilia cried, which were cool cos I got to cuddle her,' Jude revealed.

Cecilia tittered. 'Yes, I did. Your cuddles are the perfect accompaniment to *The Man Who Can't Be Moved*,' she said.

'Now I want to take Millie to a concert of sad songs so I can cuddle her,' Floyd said.

The mention of going to a concert together, which would be in the future, delighted Millie.

'Are you okay, Millie? You look deep in thought,' Floyd asked.

'Yes, I'm fine thanks. I was daydreaming about going to a concert with you and snuggling up for the heartstring-pulling songs,' Millie lied.

As it was now cool enough, Millie had a bite of her food. It was creamy, salty, delicious, and the perfect distraction.

After a dessert of cake Cecilia had bought from The Lion Walk Bakery and cream from the supermarket had been enjoyed, the quartet of friends, family, and lovers moved through to the lounge. She turned the telly on, which showed a long-haired singer on BBC One singing away the rest of the year. He was singing a song about going to space.

'Will you two finally get married next year?' Millie asked.

Jude looked at Cecilia to answer, though he knew what she'd say. 'I'm not sure. A date hasn't been set. When I proposed to Jude, I did so to show him I was serious about our relationship, not because I wanted to marry him the next day. We're saving so we can have the wedding and honeymoon we wish for without going into debt or leaving ourselves short for married life. I do promise that, one day, you'll get to be a bridesmaid,' she told Millie.

'Bridesmaid? I get to be a bridesmaid?' Millie questioned.

As they'd already known she was going to be a bridesmaid,

Floyd, Jude, and Cecilia smiled at Millie. On this occasion, Cecilia looked to Jude to answer Millie.

'Yeah, of course you're gonna be a bridesmaid. Your Floyd will be best man,' Jude confirmed.

'Best man? I'm going to be your best man?' Floyd questioned.

As they'd already known he was going to be best man, Millie, Jude, and Cecilia smiled at Floyd.

'Yeah, you're my mate,' Jude said.

'And you're like the little sister I never had,' Cecilia told Millie.

From the moment she'd met Cecilia, Millie had gotten big sister vibes from her. Her firm but caring nature made her instantly feel like family. Never had Millie imagined Cecilia felt the same about her. It touched her so much that she couldn't speak.

'What about you two? I don't suppose you're getting married next year, but do you have plans?' Jude asked.

It was the question Millie hadn't been brave enough to ask. Not a breath passed her lips as she waited for the answer.

'Yes, I have plans,' Floyd replied.

The only noise in the room was the television, on which a presenter announced there was only a minute left in the year.

The four of them spent the rest of the year with their eyes on the telly. Big black hands moved across the illuminated clock faces of Elizabeth Tower towards midnight. When they aligned, Big Ben chimed.

Fifty miles from the scenes on TV, two couples were kissing. Their kisses were soft and swift as the presence of siblings made the atmosphere far from romantic. Despite this, inside her Millie felt fireworks brighter than those being shown on the screen she was now ignoring.

32

Chapter Thirty-two

After sitting on the kitchen side overnight, dirty mugs were left unattended the following morning as Floyd overslept so had to dash out for work and Millie was lost in her textbooks. Knowing the mugs were waiting to be washed up bothered Millie so much, she struggled to concentrate on her books.

After scoffing some ham sandwiches, Millie decided to do something about it. She shoved her notebooks and textbooks to one end of the sofa and left them there. She took herself and her phone to the kitchen, texting Maddie as she walked. By the time she'd discovered the washing up liquid, which Floyd had hidden away at the back of one of the lowest cupboards, Maddie had confirmed she was free and happy for Millie to call her.

After being connected to Maddie and putting her on speakerphone, Millie explained: 'I'm washing up, which is why this isn't a video call. You don't need to see me up to my elbows in soap suds.'

'Okay. I'm holding the phone to my ear as I walk down to the bottom of the garden. You've given me the perfect excuse to get away from *her*,' Maddie replied.

When Millie ran the hot tap, she felt the heat coming off the water warm her and the room, both of which had been a little chilly. She looked through the steam out the window at the land which didn't belong to the house she was in.

'*Her*?' Millie questioned.

'Kayleigh. The cow came home for Christmas and just won't leave. She lives two doors down, and I've seen her *every* day. I know I see her every day in Cambridge, but it's worse here. I've been thinking about it for a while and have finally worked out why,' Maddie ranted.

Though Maddie's tone upset Millie, her words delighted her. They confirmed, not only were Maddie and Kayleigh not friends, but Maddie felt the same way about her as Millie.

When she remembered Maddie was waiting for an answer, Millie asked: 'What's different about seeing Kayleigh at home?'

'You're not here to cheer me up and distract me from her overfriendlyness, as you'd put it. She acts like we're best mates. Our parents are, but we're not. The girl sat next to me in class for a few years, we shared a sandwich once, and she used to have to come round mine after school when her parents worked late, but proximity and necessity don't make you friends. Kayleigh is a snob. I never knew it before, but then she talked about you and I realised,' Maddie explained.

'That's why she hates me! I'm poor!' Millie realised aloud.

'She hates you? I've got that impression this week, but how do you know?' Maddie questioned.

The words that just a month ago Millie had been unable to say tumbled out. 'Kayleigh bullies me. She waits until there's no-one around and says nasty things about my weight or being stupid,' she told Maddie.

Maddie gasped. 'Oh, Millie! Why didn't you tell me? I had no idea,' she cried.

'I was embarrassed. I thought it was my fault,' Millie explained.

'Now I *really* want to see you, so I can make it absolutely clear it isn't your fault,' Maddie said.

When Millie wiped the coffee ring out of the bottom of a mug she'd drank out of, she realised her heart was warmer than the water in the washing up bowl. She turned the hot tap on to rectify that.

'Would you come to Aylesbury, Millie? I know we'll be in Cambridge again in a week or so, but I really miss you,' Maddie asked.

In the real-world, Millie heard Maddie's voice practically begging her to leave Colchester. In her head she saw Floyd's caring brown eyes and felt his arm round her.

'I'll meet you in London, at Stratford. We can grab a bite to eat in Westfield's, hop on the tube to Marylebone, and out to my neck of the woods. I'll give you your present when you get here. I'll even buy your train ticket, as it's me that wants you to come,' Maddie told Millie.

As she placed Floyd's now-clean favourite mug on the side, Millie knew what he'd say. He'd encourage her to go and be with her friend in need. It wasn't him stopping her. She was stopping herself.

There was only the slightest doubt in Millie's mind that she and Floyd had the rest of their lives to spend together. She could afford to give up a week early in their relationship.

'I'll come, Maddie. I'll pack tomorrow so I can be with you on Friday,' Millie confirmed.

A cheer came down the phone. 'Thank you, gorgeous girl! Thank you so much! Now when she winds me up I can just breathe and remind myself that you're coming soon. I can't wait to see you, and hug you, and show you my family and Buckinghamshire. This is wonderful!' Maddie enthused.

The joy of her friend made up for the sadness Millie felt when she thought about cutting her time with Floyd short.

-

When Floyd came through the door, he was whistling. 'Guess who's got Friday off because he had to work Tuesday?' he said as he sauntered into the lounge.

The whistling stopped abruptly when Floyd saw Millie's face. 'What's up?' he asked.

'Maddie wants me to visit her. She is really sad, so I said yes. I'm leaving Friday morning. Tomorrow is our last night here. I'm so sorry,' Millie said.

'So next week I'll have the house to myself?' Floyd questioned.

'Yes, you'll be all alone. I am sorry, but this is my friend. She needs me,' Millie replied.

'Go, go help your friend. It's not what I expected, but it's great,' Floyd said.

When he saw the confusion on Millie's face, Floyd cursed himself and added: 'I mean great that you have such a strong friendship. I will miss you while we're apart, very much. You bring such warmth to the house. You're right to go though.'

A smile returned to Millie's face. Just as she'd hoped, he understood. She'd be reunited with her friend in a matter of days and, she believed, with Floyd in a week or two.

33

Chapter Thirty-three

Though her face was a little chilly, most of Millie was snuggly and toasty thanks to Nanny Millicent's blanket and Floyd. She and Floyd had decided to repeat her first night back from Maddie's party. The only differences were they were watching the live-action version of *Beauty and the Beast* instead of *Frozen*, they were *choosing* not to use the boiler, and Millie hadn't just returned from being with her best friend, but was going to see her in less than twenty-four hours.

'I'll try not to fall asleep this time,' Millie said.

The memory of Millie snoring on his shoulder made Floyd chuckle. 'If you do, I have a plumpfy shoulder for you to rest on,' he reminded her.

'It really is. I slept so well that evening on your shoulder,' Millie agreed.

'And you can again if you wish,' Floyd told Millie.

'But I don't want to miss a second. It's hard for me to believe it, but this is my last night with you in Essex,' Millie pointed out.

Emma Watson appeared on screen as Belle walking through the

village with her nose in a book, which she was singing about. The villagers contributed to the song by trading at the market and commenting on how beautiful but bizarre Belle was. The clarity of Watson's voice and her angelic tone washed over Millie and pulled her into the film.

By the time Belle was admiring the miniature windmill her father had made based on the one they used to live in, Millie had forgotten she'd been talking to Floyd. She wasn't even aware of him sitting next to her. In her mind, she was in a little French village.

In the film, Belle's father left the village for a day to sell inventions and buy a rose. He shared an emotional goodbye with his daughter before leaving her.

'It is strange that, tomorrow, you'll be in Aylesbury,' Floyd commented having been silent for a few minutes.

That dragged Millie right back into the real world. A world in which she still didn't know what Floyd had planned for them.

Before her mind lost itself in focusing on her imminent departure from Floyd and her mood spiralled down, Millie told herself to just enjoy the evening, no matter what was going to happen in the future.

As if reading her mind, Floyd put an arm round Millie and pulled her closer. She wriggled to get as comfy as possible and then allowed herself to once again lose herself in the film, this time remembering she had Floyd for company.

34

Chapter Thirty-four

Because he insisted, Millie let Floyd carry her suitcases to the station. He had the day off from work, so she may as well make use of him.

January sunshine glinted off the buildings. Colchester was at its winter finest. One of its residents, Floyd, with his soft brown eyes that said "I love you" with every gaze, was also at his best. The combination of the two made the city almost unleaveable. Leave it, Millie had to though, to see her friend.

When her eyes fell on the barriers at Colchester station, where she and Floyd had to part, Millie felt it in her heart.

'I guess I have to take these now,' Millie said in reference to her suitcases.

As if confirming this, Floyd handed over the suitcases. His hand lingered on one of the handles, so his fingers brushed Millie's. 'I love you, Millie,' he blurted out.

'I love you too,' Millie replied without question.

'Kiss for the journey?' Floyd asked.

Millie nodded. She held still and let Floyd's soft lips lock with hers and take her away. For a few seconds, they were in a wonderland of love and passion. It felt like they'd be together forever.

A call over the tannoy for a train to London Liverpool Street brought Millie back to Colchester station and reminded her she and Floyd were not going to be together forever. They were in fact about to part for goodness knows how long.

'You must go, Millie,' Floyd told her.

Every part of Millie wanted to deny that and run home with Floyd, but she knew he was right. She turned her back on him and dragged her cases to the barrier. After showing a member of staff her phone screen, she was allowed through.

With a barrier now between them, Millie and Floyd waved goodbye. Turning away from Floyd again was one of the hardest things Millie had ever had to do.

-

Bright yellow arrows on big grey signs pointed Millie towards Westfield Stratford City. She followed them out of the station to the outside world. There, to her left, were vast glass doors that led into the shopping centre in which she was to meet Maddie.

'Hey, gorgeous girl!' a voice said behind Millie.

Knowing she'd see Maddie there, Millie span round and wrapped her up in a hug.

'Oh, I've missed my Millie cuddles. You give such warm hugs. Olaf would love you,' Maddie told Millie whilst squished against her.

The mention of Olaf reminded Millie of something. 'My prezzie to you is in one of my trundly-bags,' Millie revealed.

Now she knew her present was in one of them, Maddie beamed at the suitcases. 'Would you like me to take one of them?' she offered.

'No, thank you. Floyd carried them for me in Colchester, so I'm alright with them for the rest of the journey,' Millie replied.

Together, Millie and Maddie entered the shopping centre. The noise hit Millie like a wall. It blended together to a tuneless din. If she focused, she could pick out individual voices, such as a child explaining why the minifigure they'd built in the LEGO store was the coolest ever.

With Maddie leading the way, Millie weaved her way through the throng of people to the Food Court. A semicircle of fast-food outlets surrounding utilitarian tables and chairs offered the friends respite from the crowds making their way through the centre.

'Go find a table. I'll get the food. You know where from,' Maddie told Millie.

Happy to be able to sit, Millie thanked Maddie and made her way to the nearest empty table. She dumped her suitcases underneath at the opposite end to some empty food wrappers. Then she took a seat and rested her feet.

With nothing better to do, Millie watched Maddie queue. Her friend spent her entire time waiting in line looking at her phone. This meant Maddie didn't notice someone do a double take as they walked past her.

When Maddie finally reached the counter, the young man behind it smiled at her for the duration of their encounter. Just two feet away from him, Maddie didn't notice. Fifty feet away, Millie clearly saw his smile and guessed why the previously-frowning man was suddenly so bright and cheerful. The member of staff watched Maddie take her food away before serving the next customer, who wasn't treated to his beaming smile.

Less than a minute after leaving the counter, Maddie was with Millie. She removed a box from the brown paper bag she'd carried and handed it over. Before it had been taken out of the bag, Millie had known its contents. The box of twenty chicken nuggets now in front of her proved her right.

'You know me so well!' Millie cried.

'Well enough to know that box is inaccurate,' Maddie replied.

'Inaccurate?' Millie questioned.

'It says "sharebox", but I know I won't be getting any of them,' Maddie pointed out.

Covering the box with her hands, Millie said: 'No, it doesn't! These are all mine.'

To stop herself laughing, Maddie stuffed fries in her mouth.

The atmosphere between Millie and Maddie was one they couldn't have created on the phone.

-

As they travelled on the Central Line under London, Millie and Maddie hardly exchanged a word. Neither did any of the seven-hundredish other passengers sharing the train with them.

Only when they left Marylebone on a Chiltern Railways service did Millie and Maddie resume conversation.

'My car is at the station. It'll take around twenty minutes to drive home,' Maddie told Millie.

'I'm so looking forward to seeing where you live and meeting your family,' Millie commented.

'And they're looking forward to seeing you, especially Mum. She's Miriam, by the way. Don't call her Mrs Scanlon. She appreciates respect but isn't formal,' Maddie said.

'Oh. I was just going to call her Maddie's Mum,' Millie revealed.

Maddie laughed. 'You are *gorgeous*,' she replied.

This response left Millie feeling loved and perfectly prepared to meet Maddie's family. Daydreams about Maddie's family occupied her for the rest of the journey.

35

Chapter Thirty-five

The guest bedroom Maddie had described as "small" on the drive from the station was larger than the one Millie lived in at Floyd's house. Unlike the room in Colchester, Millie's current surroundings were characterless. She sat on the bed, swinging her legs, listening for a knock at the door.

After greeting Millie on her arrival, Miriam had insisted the family invite Kayleigh over. Both Millie and Maddie protested, but Miriam had argued seeing her Cambridge housemate would help Millie settle. This was the last thing either of the girls wanted, but Millie swiftly realised Miriam was not someone to argue with. As her daughter, Maddie already knew this and gave in far quicker than her friend.

The pleasant chimes of a doorbell rang out throughout the house. They were accompanied by harsh high-pitched yipping from Trixie, the Tibetan spaniel who had previously been snuggled up quietly in the boot room.

'Can you go, Millie? She's early. Maddie and I are still getting dressed!' Miriam called from the room next to Millie's.

As the only person who hadn't felt the need to get changed for dinner, Millie made her way to the door. Paws scrabbled across the real wood floor as Trixie dashed from her bed in the boot room to Millie's side.

After bending to give Trixie a little fuss, Millie straightened and opened the door.

'Hello,' Kayleigh said as Millie opened the door.

When Kayleigh realised it was Millie she'd spoken to, she froze for a moment. The two women stared at each other. They were both working out what to say.

'You're answering the door? Already you're in your rightful place of servan...' Kayleigh began. She stopped when Millie held her hand up like she'd seen snooker refs do when watching the sport on telly with Jude. This was something Millie had never done before, so it stunned Kayleigh into silence.

At Millie's feet, Trixie was anything but silent. The little dog growled at Kayleigh, inching towards her.

'Is what you're about to say true?' Millie asked.

'Erm,' Kayleigh stammered.

'Is it good? Does it reflect positively on the person you're talking about, me in this case?' Millie questioned.

'No, but so it shouldn't,' Kayleigh replied.

'And is it useful and necessary? Do I really need to know what you're going to tell me?' Millie asked.

'It was just a comment. A witty observation,' Kayleigh said.

'Then I don't need to hear it. Please come in and, from now on, only say true, good, or useful things to me,' Millie concluded.

'Woof!' Trixie added, in total agreement with Millie.

Having dealt with Kayleigh, Millie walked away from her, followed by Trixie. Kayleigh slunk in behind them.

With perfect timing, Maddie descended the stairs in her elegant blue gown. 'Is everything alright here?' she questioned.

'Yeah, sure,' Kayleigh mumbled.

When Maddie caught Millie's eye, she beamed at her.

From behind Maddie, Miriam appeared. 'Good evening, Kayleigh. Glad you could join us,' she said.

'Well, I'm sorry Mrs Scanlon, but I won't be joining you. I'm feeling a little under the weather now, so I'm off home,' Kayleigh revealed.

It was hard for Millie to not cheer. She saw the same suppressed joy in Maddie.

There was nothing suppressed about Miriam's feelings. Warmth disappeared from her face to be replaced by confusion followed by displeasure with a hint of disappointment. 'Then get going, and call me Miriam when you text me to let you know you're home safe. I have told you that,' she ordered in a tone matching her expression.

With a muttered agreement, Kayleigh scurried through the door, slamming it on her way out.

'Do you and Kayleigh not get on, Millie?' Miriam asked.

The direct question shocked Millie more than the bang of the door closing behind Kayleigh. 'Well, it's tricksy,' Millie said.

It wasn't just Millie who was uncomfortable. 'I'm going to make us some tea,' Maddie murmured, slipping away before anyone could stop her. Trixie trotted away after her.

In the absence of her friend, Millie felt Miriam's curious gaze firmly fix on her. She worried Maddie's mum would be able to see right through her.

'Trixie is our dog. It's no way to describe your relationship with Kayleigh. I know what she's like. Her mother thinks picking on people, including her own daughter and husband, is funny. Kayleigh follows her example,' Miriam assured Millie.

'She bullies me in Cambridge,' Millie blurted out.

Shock briefly made an appearance on Miriam's face. A moment later, she composed herself. 'She's like that even at university? Maddie has never said so. I really hoped she'd change once away from her mother, but it seems not. I was so sure she was a different person in Cambridge,' she said.

This made Millie question something. 'If Maddie hasn't told you, what made you suspect things were not friendly between me and Kayleigh?' she asked.

'I wasn't born yesterday. I know Kayleigh isn't ill. If she was, she'd have text to say she wasn't coming. She only decided to go home when she saw you. It was then I began to question if she really had changed and I suspected something had happened between you two,' Miriam explained.

Millie nodded. 'I finally bested her,' she revealed.

As she returned to the hallway, Maddie caught the end of her friend's sentence. 'Who, Kayleigh? What did you say?' she questioned.

'I used Socrates three sieves,' Millie told Maddie and Miriam.

The frown on Maddie's face told Millie her friend thought she was talking about kitchenware.

'Ah, the tests of truthfulness, usefulness, and kindness, or something like that. A good idea, I've always thought. More people should think like that,' Miriam said.

Millie gasped. 'You understand! You know Socrates?' she asked.

'I do not *know* him for I am not quite *that* old, but I know *of* him. My brother took quite an interest in Ancient Greece when we were growing up. You, I understand, are a philosophy student? Come through to the lounge and let's talk about that. There's no need to give someone like Kayleigh airtime in our conversation,' Miriam suggested.

As she considered the matter settled, Miriam sauntered away from the scene of the showdown between Millie and Kayleigh towards the lounge. Maddie and Millie naturally followed, one of them skipping along, full of joy at the prospect of chatting about her favourite subject.

36

Chapter Thirty-six

A fishy scent lingered in the kitchen long after the smoked salmon and egg muffins it was from had been eaten. It was accompanied by Miriam and her husband, Aaron, making plans for the day.

'Are you two alright to stay here? I don't imagine you wish to come to Waitrose with us,' Aaron asked.

It stunned Millie so much that the family shopped at Waitrose, she didn't answer.

'We'll be fine. I'll take a walk down the garden with Millie,' Maddie replied.

The scrabbling of paws on hard floors announced Trixie's arrival in the kitchen.

'Okay, Millie, *Trixie*, and I will take a walk down the garden,' Maddie corrected.

Satisfied their daughter, their dog, and her friend would be okay home alone, Miriam and Aaron headed out. They called goodbye to Millie as they left and didn't get a response.

'Would you like to see where I go when I want to call you and need privacy?' Maddie asked.

'Yes,' Millie replied.

Though there was no enthusiasm in Millie's voice, it didn't deter Maddie. She headed off to the boot room and returned with her North Face waterproof jacket and the only coat Millie had brought with her.

'We'll leave by the kitchen door. It rained last night, and the slope down from the boot room is lethal when wet,' Maddie said.

As she was thinking about how incredible it was that Maddie's home had two different doors to the garden and Floyd's house didn't even have a garden, Millie didn't answer.

The kitchen door led out to a granite-paved patio. Millie pointed up to the wooden structure covering it and commented: 'I like this slatty-boxy thing.'

'Ah, the pergola? Yes, we like that too. It provides shade in summer. Dad used to do legendary barbecues for the August bank holiday. Our little tibbie here loved the titbits guests used to drop for her,' Maddie replied.

Slabs of limestone placed at random intervals led across a grass lawn. Millie followed Maddie and Trixie through a gap in the hedge at the end of the path and found yet more garden on the other side. A grass slope led down to a fence that prevented Maddie and her family from falling into the stream beyond.

'This is where I come to call you,' Maddie told Millie, gesturing at the stream.

'It's beautiful, and this is your home. You own this garden,' Millie sighed.

'We're very lucky. Please don't ever think I don't know how lucky I am. My parents worked very hard to give me this life. I appreciate it more than I can say,' Maddie said.

Though her rented family home was far smaller than Maddie's, and the Austens lacked many of the luxuries the Scanlon family had, Millie was just as grateful as her friend. The love her parents had given her was priceless.

'There used to be raised vegetable beds here. I remember sowing carrot seeds with Mum and staring at the bed as if I expected them to pop up out of the soil immediately,' Maddie revealed.

Millie giggled. 'I grew carrots too! Nanny Millicent had an allotment that she took me down to,' she cried.

'And did *you* expect them to grow instantly?' Maddie asked.

'Yes. I was disappointed when they didn't. Nanny told me off for being impatient, but she did it with that kind love-you-really smile on her face,' Millie replied.

The friends laughed together. Some ducks drifting down the stream beyond the fence quacked along with their laughter.

'I never knew either of my nans. Mum's mum died before my parents met. *Dad's* mum didn't like *my* mum, something to do with her not having enough money, even though Mum now earns more than Dad, so my paternal grandparents disowned us all,' Maddie told Millie.

Suddenly Maddie found herself wrapped up in a Millie hug. She returned it, holding her friend close. When their eyes met, Millie squeezed Maddie as tightly as she could, as if trying to share as much love as possible.

'You give the best hugs,' Maddie whispered.

After kissing Maddie on the cheek, Millie tried to let her go, but Maddie held on. Millie loved hugs and had only attempted to end this one because she thought she ought to. She happily embraced Maddie for another minute, letting her body heat banish the crisp January air.

When Maddie released her, Millie realised she was crying. 'I've always wanted more family. As you know, I have an uncle and a few cousins, but they lived in Scotland when I was growing up, so

I didn't see them. It's just Mum and Dad, who are lovely, but that made for a lonely childhood. No siblings to play with or grandparents to visit. I didn't even have many friends. That's how I got stuck with Kayleigh,' Maddie said.

'Oh, poor girl,' Millie murmured.

Trixie jumped up at her crying owner. This prompted Maddie to crouch down and stroke the little dog.

'I think of it every Christmas, because our table is so small. Now though, it's a little easier, because I have the sister I've always dreamt of,' Maddie continued, running her hand through Trixie's soft fur.

Millie gasped. 'Oh, is Miriam pregnant? Congratulations!' she cried.

This assumption brought a smile to Maddie's lips. 'No, Mum isn't pregnant. I'm not related to my new sister,' she corrected.

'So your parents are adopting? That's great! Good for them,' Millie replied.

Now Maddie was so amused that she laughed. 'No, you've got the wrong end of the stick. Gorgeous girl, I'm talking about *you*. You're like a sister to me,' she explained.

As soon as Maddie said it, Millie realised she was right. Millie loved her in the same way she loved Jude. That made them siblings, even if their parents had never even met.

'And you are the sister *I* always wished for. I adore my brothers, especially Jude, but they are boys. I wanted a sister too, and now I have one. Two really, because Cecilia is like a sister too,' Millie agreed.

'Sisters forever?' Maddie asked, straitening up and holding her hand out to shake.

As she took Maddie's hand, Millie replied: 'Sisters forever.'

When Maddie realised she'd forgotten something, she gasped. 'Sisters exchange presents at Christmas!' she cried.

The excitement of seeing Maddie's house and meeting her family had made Millie forget about presents too. That was something she hadn't thought was possible. 'Yay, prezzies! I love prezzies. We must go inside immediately and open them,' Millie enthused.

-

The first present opened was Millie's to Maddie. Maddie peeled the sticky tape off the glittery bundle and opened up the paper to reveal a dress. As the dress was folded, Maddie couldn't fully appreciate it. She stood and held it out in front of her, smiling when it unfurled.

'It reminded the lady helping me shop of Princess Anna's dress,' Millie revealed.

'And I can see why. This dress is fit for a Disney princess,' Maddie replied.

'It is imperfect. That's how I was able to buy it,' Millie told Maddie.

'You bought it for me, therefore it is perfect,' Maddie argued.

Unwilling to reject a compliment, Millie said nothing more. She just let Maddie stroke the velvet of her new dress.

Once she'd had enough of holding the dress, Maddie told Millie she was going to take it safely to her room and bring down her presents. The wording, presents *plural*, both excited and embarrassed Millie.

The two presents Maddie carried into the room a minute later were both wrapped in sophisticated grey paper scattered with metallic silver stars. As soon as one of them was handed to Millie, she tore it open, shredding the paper to bits in her haste. This revealed a pair of white fluffy mules. Millie put one on her hand as if it was a glove and felt the memory foam sole mould to the shape of her palm.

'I bought you outdoor shoes, boots, for your birthday, so it seemed appropriate to buy indoor shoes, slippers, for Christmas. Also, they are sort-of related to my other present,' Maddie explained.

'I love them. They feel so luxurious,' Millie whispered.

'If you think slippers are luxurious, wait until you open this,' Maddie said, handing over a present not much thicker or bigger than a letter.

As she'd been told to, Millie opened her second present. Inside she found an envelope. 'Well, I do love stationery. Thanks, Maddie,' she commented.

'Open the envelope,' Maddie told Millie.

After ripping the envelope open, Millie pulled out an A5 piece of card. She read the embossed gold script and discovered it was a voucher for a spa experience for two at a Cambridge hotel.

'This is too much!' Millie cried.

Maddie tutted. 'Nothing is too much for you. You're my sister, remember?' she argued.

'I've never done anything like this. It must have been so expensive. This is worth far more than my present,' Millie pointed out.

'It's an experience for two, and I'm your plus one, unless there's someone you'd rather take. This buys me time with you, which is priceless. Please don't feel bad, Millie. We've already established that I know I'm lucky to be so privileged financially. Please let me share it,' Maddie replied.

This was enough to allay Millie's guilt. 'We're going to have such a good time,' she said.

Already dreaming of the massage she was going to have, Maddie declared: 'It will be the perfect treat for us both.'

37

Chapter Thirty-seven

It concerned Miriam and Aaron that their guest would be bored cooped up indoors all day. Millie tried to assure them she was there to see Maddie and perfectly happy, but still Aaron seemed unsure. When Maddie walked in on this discussion, she told her parents she'd take Millie out the next day. That was how Millie had ended up next to Maddie pootling along the A41 as it carved its way through the Buckinghamshire countryside.

'They would never have given in. Once Mum and Dad have an idea in their head, it's stuck there,' Maddie told Millie as she turned off the busy A road.

'I have got that impression, especially from Miriam,' Millie replied with a grin.

'Still, I'm happy. It gives me an excuse to show you a nice local landmark and play Disney soundtracks on our way,' Maddie commented.

After leaving the A road, Maddie slowed down significantly. Millie noticed her tense up when the road narrowed or swept round a bend. It was in stark contrast to the way some people Millie knew drove.

When Maddie realised Millie was watching her closely, she said: 'Sorry. I really am a city girl. These country lanes scare me.'

'Never be sorry for admitting a difficulty. We are in no rush. Take as long as you need. The completion of the task matters more than the duration of it,' Millie replied.

As she crept round a bend, Maddie thought about what Millie had said. 'That's very profound. You really are clever,' she commented.

'I'm a philosophy student. Clever words is what I do,' Millie told her friend.

'But you can't teach someone how to be clever; only how to use their cleverness,' Maddie pointed out.

Using her cleverness, Millie realised the best way to help Maddie navigate the country lanes was to stay quiet and let her concentrate.

~

When Maddie parked her car, Millie spotted the little windmill they'd gone to see.

'That's pretty,' Millie commented.

'I like the view,' Maddie replied.

So Maddie could show Millie the view, they both got out of the car and stood with their backs to the windmill and the village they'd driven through.

'To the left is Oxfordshire, and to the right, Buckinghamshire. I suggest you look to the right,' Maddie told Millie.

'Yes, who would want to look at Oxfordshire when Buckinghamshire is near?' Millie agreed.

The pair gazed in silence at Maddie's home county. Rolling hills stretched out as far as Millie could see. She let her gaze wander across the green fields. The peaceful viewpoint over simple scenery calmed her.

'This is brilliant,' Millie sighed.

'Oh, not you as well! Don't you know everyone has made that joke?' Maddie asked.

'What?' Millie questioned.

'Don't act all sweet and innocent. You know perfectly well what,' Maddie replied.

'No, I really don't,' Millie assured her.

'So you didn't read any of the signs on the way here?' Maddie asked.

'No,' Millie confirmed.

It was inconceivable to Maddie to have no idea where you were. She then thought about the fact Millie didn't drive, so had no need to know her location, and reconsidered. Her friend's cluelessness warmed her heart.

'This behind us is Brill windmill,' Maddie explained.

Only then did it dawn on Millie what Maddie was saying. 'You thought I was making a terrible pun about the name of the place? I get it now!' Millie cried.

A few other visitors who had been admiring the view around brilliant Brill windmill wandered off into the village, leaving Maddie and Millie alone.

'I'm pleased your parents pushed us out. What a beautiful place this is,' Millie commented.

'I'm pleased too. There's something I've wanted to talk to you about, but I haven't wanted to bring it up around my parents,' Maddie replied.

'What's that?' Millie asked.

'I want to ask about Floyd. I need to know how things are going there. Is he coming to Cambridge? Do I need to buy a hat?' Maddie explained.

The way Millie's eyes lit up at the mention of Floyd's name told Maddie what sort of answer to expect. 'I *love* him. Being with you is great fun, but I was so sad to leave him early. I've missed him from the moment my train pulled out of Colchester,' Millie revealed.

Maddie's placed a hand on her heart that was bursting with love. 'This is wonderful! Is he coming to Cambridge then, or will you have to put up with a long-distance relationship for a while?' she asked.

'I don't know,' Millie admitted.

For the first time since reuniting with Millie in Stratford, Maddie frowned. 'What do you mean? Haven't you two talked about the future?' she questioned.

'Well, no. This is Floyd. He likes surprises,' Millie said.

The serious tone of their conversation had drawn Millie and Maddie's attention away from the view and towards each other. Both their brows were furrowed. Their mouths were curved firmly down.

'Gorgeous girl, I hate to say this, but I have doubts. This should have been talked about. If you love each other, you have to plan your future together,' Maddie replied.

'Floyd is planning our future, I'm sure of it. I'll go back to Cambridge in a week and he'll be there on our doorstep,' Millie declared, full of confidence.

'I'm not so sure. If that's the case, why hasn't he told you?' Maddie questioned.

'Like I said, he likes surprising me. He'd never tell me where we were going on dates. This is all a romantic game,' Millie insisted.

Maddie shook her head. 'I hope you're right,' she murmured.

'I am right! This is Floyd, and this is what he does! I love him, he loves me, and we'll all be happy and drink tea!' Millie snapped.

To hide the peculiar mix of concern at Floyd's lack of clarity, hurt due to Millie's tone, and amusement thanks to her rhyming words that Maddie felt, she turned towards Oxfordshire. She was forced to admit to herself it was virtually indistinguishable from her native Buckinghamshire.

As it was clear Maddie had no answer, Millie gazed out at Buckinghamshire. Clouds were blocking the sun, making the scene a lot darker than it had been. The change in the weather reflected Millie's feelings about her and Floyd. She'd stopped questioning whether she had a future with him. All she'd felt unsure of was what a shared future would look like. Now she wondered if her best friend had a point.

It then occurred to Millie that Maddie could be in on Floyd's plans. It was possible she'd planted seeds of doubt on his orders to make it even better when Floyd revealed his plans.

Now she had a theory to explain Maddie's behaviour, Millie wasn't so cross with her. She therefore wanted to chat to her again. To reopen conversation, Millie told her: 'It's sweet of you to not mention Floyd around Miriam and Aaron, but I don't mind them knowing about him.'

'It wasn't just for you that I didn't mention him. If I talk about relationships, Mum will once again ask why I'm single,' Maddie revealed.

'My mum also expects me to already have my love life sorted. That's normal. It's because they care about us,' Millie pointed out.

Maddie sighed. 'I know, and that's lovely, but I don't want to talk about that with her. I don't *want* to be single. Waking up alone makes me sad. It isn't through lack of trying, either. You know how much I date. I don't need Mum to remind me that I'm failing at love,' she explained.

'You are not failing. There is no rush to find your special someone. You don't even have to have a special someone. The completion of the task matters more than the duration of it,' Millie told her friend.

The familiar words pulled Maddie out of the dark hole her thinking had fallen into. 'Thank you, gorgeous girl. You are absolutely right. There is no rush to find love,' she agreed.

Wind howled across the rolling hills Millie and Maddie had been admiring and whipped round them and Brill Windmill. As the brake was on, the sails of the windmill didn't turn. As they were cold, Millie and Maddie both shivered.

'There might be a rush to get out of that though,' Millie commented.

'Shall we shelter in the pub we passed on the way in?' Maddie suggested.

'To the pub!' Millie agreed as wind propelled them in that direction.

38

Chapter Thirty-eight

Studying helped keep doubts about Floyd out of Millie's mind, but they returned the moment she put her books down. It was made harder by the complete lack of contact with him. He hadn't messaged her since the day she'd arrived in Buckinghamshire. Her fight against the urge to call Floyd lasted a few days. The knowledge that it was the weekend, so Floyd definitely wouldn't be working, overwhelmed her self-control.

The moment Millie gave in, she was eating breakfast with Maddie and Miriam. As soon as she'd scoffed her penultimate piece of chewy sourdough toast, Millie excused herself by announcing she wanted to feed her last slice to the ducks in the stream beyond the fence. On her walk down the garden, Millie messaged Maddie to tell her she was calling Floyd.

On the third ring, Floyd answered. 'Hi,' he said, his tone breathy.

After over a week out of touch, Millie had expected more than "Hi". Whilst being cross about this, she noticed Floyd was panting.

'I miss you,' Millie blurted out. It was the primary thought in her mind, overwhelming curiosity and anger.

'I miss you too, so much,' Floyd replied, still panting.

'Why haven't you been in touch?' Millie asked.

'I've erm, been busy,' Floyd mumbled.

'*Too busy for the girl you love, who you called cute and clever?*' Millie thought.

There were no ducks in the stream. Millie decided to eat the slice of toast she'd brought for them, as they hadn't had the decency to swim by and cheer her up. It was probably for the best. Bread was unhealthy for ducks. Bread was also unhealthy for humans, but she didn't care about that.

'Why haven't you messaged?' Floyd questioned.

It hadn't occurred to Millie her question would be reflected back on her. 'I wanted you to message first, or call. Your texts make me smile. It's more romantic when you call or text me,' she answered.

'Then I'm really sorry that I haven't. Your texts make me smile too. I promise to be really romantic in future,' Floyd said.

Excitement made Millie almost choke on her toast. Floyd had mentioned the future! That was all she wanted.

'*When* will you be more romantic, and *where*? When will I see you again?' Millie asked.

'Erm, sorry, gotta go. Love you,' Floyd replied hastily.

Before Millie could tell Floyd she loved him too, he hung up. The joy Millie had felt when Floyd had promised to be more romantic in the future faded. Maybe he wasn't talking about her. It was possible he meant he'd be more romantic in a future relationship with someone else. He was definitely avoiding her. Was it that he didn't know how to tell her things were over between them?

The call left Millie with no appetite. She lobbed her remaining toast into the river.

'There are no ducks,' Maddie pointed out, making Millie jump by appearing behind her.

'I know that,' Millie sighed.

'You also don't have a coat,' Maddie said, handing Millie her coat.

'I did *not* know that. Thank you,' Millie replied, taking her coat and putting it on.

'I only knew because Trixie kept whining at the boot room door,' Maddie revealed, nodding at the little dog by her feet.

The friends watched Millie's toast bob down the stream in silence. Millie recalled Maddie stroking Trixie during a difficult conversation. She crouched down and the little dog trotted into her waiting hands for a fuss. 'Good little tibbie,' Millie murmured.

'So, conversation with Floyd didn't go well then?' Maddie asked.

Millie nodded. 'He was short with me and swervy when I asked questions. Don't say I told you so,' she said.

'It is not a sister's role to point out that they were right. I hoped I wasn't,' Maddie replied.

In the back of Millie's mind, a quiet voice pointed out Maddie might be wrong. Floyd had hinted they'd see each other again, and he had told Millie he loved her. With every stroke of Trixie's fur, Millie amplified the voice that believed in Floyd. The alternative, accepting their relationship really was over, was unacceptable.

'Maybe you're not right. He hasn't broken up with me,' Millie pointed out.

Maddie shrugged. 'Perhaps, but I doubt it. Please don't get your hopes up only for them to be dashed. I'm just trying to let you down gently,' she begged Millie.

It was clear to Millie talking about her relationship with Floyd any more would damage her relationship with Maddie. A change of subject was required.

As she was having similar thoughts, Maddie mentioned: 'Mum

and Dad want takeaway tonight. They can't decide between Chinese and Italian.'

'Oh, pizza. It has to be pizza. Chinese has far too much veg in it to be proper takeaway,' Millie replied.

'Then lets go and tell them,' Maddie said, taking Millie's arm and leading her back to the house.

-

As soon as Millie made the point about there being too much veg in Chinese food for it to be considered a proper takeaway, Miriam conceded. Having been told she could order whatever she wanted when the time came, Millie spent the rest of the afternoon pondering how many toppings a person could reasonably have on a pizza.

39

Chapter Thirty-nine

When Millie saw Maddie was wearing a burgundy velvet dress, she gasped. Though Maddie had claimed to love it when she'd opened it, Millie hadn't expected her to wear it.

'You look just like a Disney princess,' Millie commented.

'I feel like one too. It seemed only right to return to Cambridge in style,' Maddie replied.

As she looked around the spacious kitchen-diner with its island, breakfast bar that the family were sat at, oak dining table, and quartz worktops, Millie wasn't sad her time in Buckinghamshire was coming to an end. In their Cambridge shared house, she felt equal to Maddie. They were both students. It was their brains that mattered, not their wallets. In the Scanlon's Buckinghamshire home, it was impossible to ignore how wealthy Maddie and her family were.

'Thank you for coming, Millie. It's been a pleasure to get to know my daughter's best friend,' Miriam said.

Inside, Millie glowed brighter than the spotlights shining down on her. 'Thank *you*, Miriam. You've been a lovely host. I've felt welcome here,' Millie told her.

'Anyone Maddie likes is welcome here. Maybe one day she'll come home with someone she *loves*,' Miriam commented.

Maddie shovelled omelette into her mouth so she couldn't answer.

'Maybe. Maybe she won't. If she doesn't bring a boy home next Christmas, blame me. Maddie and I spend every minute we're not studying together. We have no time for boys,' Millie replied.

'When we met, at uni, it took me ages to get close to you because your friends were always around. It wasn't until years after we'd graduated, when we were quite a bit older than our Maddie, that we got a moment to ourselves and I plucked up the courage to ask you out,' Aaron pointed out.

There was a pause whilst Miriam worked out how to answer that. 'I guess. We married a bit later in our lives than the average at that time,' she conceded.

'Love can come at any age,' Millie added.

'Yes,' Miriam murmured.

Aaron clapped his hands together. 'Right, time to head off,' he declared.

When Miriam was out of the way, getting shoes from her bedroom, Maddie, Millie, and Aaron shared a grin to congratulate themselves for their silent teamwork.

~

The drive to Cambridge was uneventful. Millie spent most of it gazing out the window wondering what would have been going through Maddie's mind the first time she'd travelled to Cambridge. On Millie's first trip, her dad had driven and Jude had held her hand the whole way. He'd shared her excitement on the journey, but hadn't instantly fallen in love with the city like she had.

There was no driveway outside the shared student house, so Aaron pulled up on the road when they reached Cambridge. As soon as the car had stopped, Millie jumped out and dashed to her front door.

'She's happy to be home,' Miriam commented.

'Because she thinks someone is here waiting for her!' Maddie realised out loud.

Whilst making the point to Miriam that love wasn't something to be rushed, Millie had realised how impatient she was. She wanted to be with Floyd, and she wanted to be with him that instant. Her heart knew, no matter what Maddie said, Floyd would be there for her in Cambridge, and everywhere she went for the rest of her life.

'Hello! I'm home!' Millie called as she opened the door.

No answer came.

The silence made Millie realise Floyd couldn't be in the house as he didn't have a key. She looked down at her feet to see if he'd posted a note through the door. There was nothing there.

Footsteps on the first floor made Millie's heart soar. She leapt up the stairs and almost walked into Kayleigh at the top of them.

'Is he here? Has my Floyd come?' Millie asked.

The only response Kayleigh gave was a cold stare.

'Please, Kayleigh, tell me if you've seen Floyd. It's important!' Millie pleaded.

Kayleigh shrugged. 'I've got nothing true, nice, or useful to say,' she told Millie.

Having answered Millie, Kayleigh shoved past her and trudged down the stairs. At the bottom of them, Maddie shoved past her.

'He's not here,' Millie said.

'I know, gorgeous girl, I know,' Maddie murmured, putting her arm round Millie.

'Why? Doesn't he love me?' Millie questioned, her voice high and squeaky.

Using the arm that was already around Millie's shoulders, Maddie guided her friend towards her bedroom door. She used her free hand to unlock it and close it behind them once they were through.

Once inside Maddie's room, Millie automatically sank down onto her bed and started crying.

'I don't know why he isn't here. I don't know if he loves you. I *do* know that *I* love you,' Maddie told Millie.

'Yes, but not kissy-cuddly love. That's what I thought Floyd and I had,' Millie replied.

A voice called Maddie from downstairs. She sighed and said: 'I need to get our bags so Mum and Dad can go. I'll be back.'

As she plodded down the stairs, Maddie silently cursed Floyd. Millie wore her heart on her sleeve. He had to know how much he was hurting her.

'Ah, did Millie find who she was looking for?' Miriam asked her daughter when she returned to the car.

'No. He's let her down. She sends her apologies for her absence and has asked me to thank you for having her,' Maddie replied.

'What a shame not to say goodbye. Still, we loved having Millie. I'd be happy for her to return to Bucks one day,' Miriam said.

At that moment in time, Maddie wasn't sure if Millie would return to the world outside her bedroom, let alone Buckinghamshire.

40

Chapter Forty

The one sentence reply played over and over in Millie's head. "Glad to hear it," Floyd had said, when Millie had told him she was safely back in her Cambridge bed.

In Millie's Cambridge bed with her was Maddie, who'd brought ice cream and two spoons. They'd shared the contents of the tub, both aware Millie was getting the majority, and watched *Frozen II* together. As Millie had fallen asleep on her, Maddie remained with Millie throughout the night.

-

The pure joy of ice cream and an unplanned sleepover ensured Millie spent the first few minutes of her day laughing. The sadness of Floyd's absence dragged her mood down when Maddie left her to get dressed in private, but it didn't crush her like it had on the previous day.

Once they were reunited at the breakfast table, which they had to themselves, Maddie asked: 'How are you?'

'Full of crossness, but I'll cope,' Millie replied.

'It is awful that he's hardly speaking to you, and hasn't even had the decency to properly break up with you,' Maddie agreed.

'The crossness is directed at myself,' Millie corrected.

The slice of toast Maddie had been about to eat was set back down on her plate. 'Why?' Maddie questioned.

'Because Floyd never promised me anything. He never said he'd be here. He never said we were more than a holiday romance. I assumed. All I've lost is a fantasy of my own making,' Millie explained.

After opening her mouth to protest, Maddie swiftly closed it having not spoken a word. There was too much truth in Millie's statement to dismiss it.

Though Maddie hadn't spoken a word, Millie knew what she was thinking. She smiled at her and continued to eat her toast.

~

When there was nothing but crumbs on her plate, Millie rose to her feet. This prompted Maddie to raise her eyebrows. The evident concern in her friend's eyes touched Millie.

'Don't worry, Maddie. I'll lose myself in my studies, which you know I love, and will focus on the good bits when he comes to mind. My degree means so much to me. I won't let this derail me,' Millie assured her friend.

'I'm more concerned about your heart than a fancy piece of paper,' Maddie replied.

'I have you, Maddie, and my sister-in-law-to-be. I'll be fine,' Millie pointed out.

Being in the same list as Millie's future sister-in-law delighted Maddie. They really were as like sisters as two girls could be without sharing parents.

Thinking of actual siblings made Maddie question something. 'Why isn't Jude on that list?' she asked.

'If I tell him about how things with Floyd have gone, he'll kill him with a paint tray,' Millie explained.

'A paint tray?' Maddie questioned.

'You can kill someone with a tray, if you hack at them with the thin bit,' Millie assured Maddie.

Splutters of laughter escaped Maddie. 'Well, yes. I was just thinking that a paint tray is an odd murder weapon,' she said

'Jude is a painter and decorator. He wouldn't waste a tray on killing someone though. He needs a tray,' Millie explained.

As she knew this was all the sense she'd get out of Millie, Maddie didn't continue the odd discussion.

'Anyway, I must prepare for a day's study,' Millie said.

'Would you like to take any mini-chocolates with you? My parents gave us Celebrations as a welcome back gift,' Maddie asked.

'Erm, Twix please,' Millie agreed.

After giving Millie the caramel and biscuit mini-chocolate she'd requested, Maddie hugged her. She kissed her forehead too, hoping the extra affection would help her friend get through the day.

41

Chapter Forty-one

Though it was a day shorter than average, having started on the Tuesday, Millie's first week back at Cambridge University dragged. All she wanted was to get to the weekend when she could lay in bed all day and have a good cry. It had been harder to concentrate than she had ever imagined possible. Her mind flitted between blaming herself for what had become of her relationship with Floyd, blaming him, and blaming no-one but being sad about what had happened. Even after all the disappointments, having received no sign Floyd would ever even text her again, let alone turn up in Cambridge, at times it was hard for Millie to truly believe he wasn't about to knock on the door.

Before crying in her room, Millie headed downstairs for a bowl of cereal. Maddie wasn't there, but Kayleigh was. That meant she was virtually guaranteed a silent breakfast. Kayleigh really had not said anything that wasn't true, good, or useful since Millie had returned. That hadn't left her with much to say.

Supermarket's own cornflakes tinkled into a bowl when Millie tipped the big box up. A smile crossed her lips as she thought about a certain John Harvey Kellogg. He'd invented cornflakes to stop people masturbating, or at least to stop them wanting to. They were meant to be an anti-aphrodisiac. As a philosophy student, Millie was used to reading strange ideas like that. As a woman who imagined herself single for a long time now, Millie wondered if she should eat cornflakes to quell the natural urges she'd have.

Though she didn't believe they'd have any impact on her libido, and she didn't really want them to anyway, Millie enjoyed her crunchy cornflakes.

Just as Millie shovelled the last mouthful of cornflakes into her mouth, there was a knock at the door. Kayleigh, who'd finished her breakfast biscuit, left the room to answer it, leaving a trail of crumbs in her wake.

Someone spoke to Kayleigh when she opened the door. The voice was too distant for Millie to make out their words.

After closing the door, Kayleigh returned to the kitchen-diner and told Millie: 'A man called Floyd is at the door for you.'

Millie gasped. 'How could you say that? I know you're cruel, but that's a new level of nastiness!' she cried.

'Cruel? I'm passing on a message. If a man, or anyone actually, turned up on my doorstep and told me they loved me, which has never happened in my entire life because no-one loves me, I think I'd be eternally grateful to the person who'd told me, not accuse them of "nastiness",' Kayleigh ranted.

'Don't talk like it's true. Don't get my hopes up like that. I know you're lying,' Millie snapped back.

Kayleigh stormed out of the room in a huff. The fact she didn't answer in words confirmed to Millie her housemate had indeed been lying.

As she'd made a New Year's resolution not to cry when Kayleigh said or did nasty things, Millie kept her pain inside. It took all her effort to do this, so she didn't hear Kayleigh throw the front door open again or clomp up the stairs.

Only when someone hugged her did Millie become aware of the world outside her mind again. Sadness was replaced by a familiar warmth.

'Oh, Millie. I hoped you'd be happy that I'd come to see you,' Floyd murmured into her ear.

'Floyd. My Floyd. You're hugging me,' Millie realised out loud.

After giving Millie a big squeeze, Floyd withdrew so he could look into her grey eyes. They weren't as soft or warm as he remembered.

'Why didn't you tell me you were coming? Why have you hardly spoken to me for ages?' Millie asked, her tone sharper than Floyd had ever heard.

'It's all meant to be a surprise. I've been planning in secret for ages,' Floyd explained.

Rage and love filled Millie. They were released together in a playful punch of Floyd's coat-covered shoulder. 'You silly-Floydy! I thought you didn't want me anymore,' Millie snapped.

Discomfort in his shoulder made Floyd recoil. 'Ow, that hurt! I never meant to give you the idea that I didn't love you. All I wanted was to surprise you,' he told Millie.

'Oh, and I didn't mean to hurt you! Sorry,' Millie replied.

A curious and slightly apprehensive Floyd watched Millie approach the shoulder she'd punched, head bent. He wondered if she was going to headbutt it too to add to the pain. That wasn't what Millie did. She laid a gentle kiss on his slightly-uncomfortable shoulder.

'There, kiss it better,' Millie said.

'You are so cute, and I am so in love with you,' Floyd told Millie.

'And I am in love with you, though you aren't cute, but I am also very cross,' Millie replied.

With her sweet voice, Millie didn't sound at all cross to Floyd. He didn't doubt she was though. Even when cross, Millie was adorable.

From a deep coat pocket, Floyd pulled out a white paper bag that he handed to Millie. 'I had to come to give you these. You are on your period again, so in need of something sweet,' he explained.

'A bag of cookies with my name on!' Millie cried.

When she caught the smile on Floyd's face, Millie added: 'But I'm still cross.'

'Why don't we go for a walk together? The fresh January breeze might blow away your crossness, as you'd probably call it, and I can explain why I've been so distant,' Floyd suggested.

Millie nodded enthusiastically. 'Yes, please!' she agreed.

After Millie had put her coat on to keep her toasty, she and Floyd headed out the door. She tried very hard not to smile at him as he took her hand to lead her into Cambridge, but it was an impossible task. He was as irresistible as ever.

42

Chapter Forty-two

For the first minute or so, Millie and Floyd plodded along in silence. He then asked her how staying with Maddie had been. She spoke at length about how it had been like visiting a beloved sister and how beautiful Buckinghamshire was, although posh. To Floyd she was able to admit being in such luxurious surroundings made her uncomfortable.

When talking about Maddie, Millie remembered how she'd desperately tried to get her to accept Floyd was no longer interested in a relationship and she should let him go. Maddie had been especially passionate after Millie's brief call with Floyd in which he'd hung up on her.

'I called you whilst I was with Maddie and you barely said two words to me. You cut me off to avoid answering a question,' Millie reminded Floyd.

Floyd grimaced. 'Yes, that. That was a packing day. I'd avoided messaging you so I didn't give the game away and I was so nervous that it was all just going to slip out,' he explained.

'Nervous that *what* was going to slip out?' Millie asked.

There was a pause whilst Millie and Floyd waited to cross a road. Cyclists nipping across their path at great speed took all their concentration.

Once safely across the road, Millie paused. It wasn't necessary for her to tell Floyd this was her way of demanding an explanation.

'I'm moving, Millie, or rather I *have* moved. That's why I was packing up boxes in what was our Colchester home,' Floyd revealed.

One of the few things Millie knew about Floyd's parents was they'd emigrated to France. So had his aunt and uncle. The only relative he had in Britain was a cousin. That meant it wasn't hard to guess where Floyd was going.

'Oh. *Bon voyage*, I guess,' Millie said.

'I've already moved. It was a little stressful, but so worth it. I like my new flat,' Floyd told her.

Millie sighed. 'Then I'm happy for you. *La vie est belle* and all that,' she replied.

'Life *is* beautiful, but why are you speaking in French all of a sudden?' Floyd questioned.

'Because that's where you're going, isn't it? You've returned to England to tell me you're leaving me. This is *au revoir*!' Millie cried.

Now he understood Millie's confusion, Floyd smiled. 'I've moved to Waterbeach,' he revealed.

'That's not France,' Millie realised out loud.

'No. It's about six miles away. Just a couple of stops away on the train. Close enough, but affordable, unlike this entire city, which must be the most expensive place in England outside London,' Floyd confirmed.

Giggles erupted from Millie. 'I can come and stay. We can have naughty sleepovers,' she said.

'Naughty sleepovers?' Floyd questioned.

'Yes, I can spend the night with you and we can have sex,' Millie explained, getting quieter with every word.

Floyd grinned. 'I see,' he replied.

'Cornflakes really don't work,' Millie commented.

The comment about cornflakes made no sense to Floyd. He could question it, but decided not to. He just thought of it as one of the adorably strange things Millie said.

There were many more things Floyd had to say, and other places he had to be, so he led Millie across a lush green expanse of grass that had been perfectly mowed. It reminded him of football pitches.

Parker's Piece, which Millie was wandering across with Floyd, was lined with leafless trees. At that time of year, their future looked bleak. She knew though, in the summer, they'd be leafy and green. A day ago, she'd thought her relationship with Floyd was like a tree in winter. Now it looked more like a tree in spring, when everything comes back to life.

'I know someone from Waterbeach, but he's not talked much about home. What is it like?' Millie asked.

'There are lots of pubs and dogs there. That's all I know so far,' Floyd replied.

'So you've moved somewhere you don't really know?' Millie questioned.

'I know you're nearby. That's all I need to know,' Floyd said.

The love that conveyed made Millie skip across the rest of Parker's Piece.

~

Trumpington Street was packed full of pedestrians, disturbingly-fast-moving cyclists, and motor vehicles. Millie knew this, for she lived in Cambridge. Floyd knew this, as he was one of the pedestrians. Floyd hadn't revealed his destination, so he and Millie were wandering around Cambridge. Trumpington Street was one of the main streets in the city centre, so they'd ended up on it, as had dozens of other people.

As they reached the point where Trumpington Street met King's Parade, Floyd heard music. A glance up the road suggested it was coming from a rubbish bin in which a man was playing a guitar and singing.

'There's a man in a bin playing a guitar!' Floyd cried.

'Yes,' Millie confirmed.

'Seriously?' Floyd questioned.

'This is Cambridge,' Millie explained.

It comforted Floyd to see people muttering to each other about the man in a bin and taking their phones out to film him. Millie also took her phone out, but not to film the man. She was answering a phone call.

'That cow of a woman is saying you had a go at her. Obviously, I've told her that's utter rubbish, but what the hell *did* happen, and where are you? Her version of the story is that Floyd actually turned up on the doorstep, but when she told you, you called her a liar,' Maddie asked the second Millie answered.

'I'm near King's College, with Floyd. What Kayleigh says is true,' Millie confirmed.

It took Maddie a few seconds to absorb this. 'I don't know what to be more shocked by, her telling the truth or him turning up!' she cried.

'Both shocked me too. I was very snappy with Kayleigh. Please tell her I'll apologise for my nastiness when I get back,' Millie replied.

'Oh, bless you, gorgeous girl. She's never apologised to you, but I'll pass that on. On the subject of apologies, has someone else said sorry for being a, well, a not very nice man?' Maddie asked.

'He is a *lovely* man. He's just a silly-Floydy. I've told him so,' Millie assured Maddie.

'Well, as long as he knows I've wanted to kill him at times.

Anyway, if you two are together, I'll let you go. I know you'll tell me all about it when you get back,' Maddie said.

Whilst Floyd filmed the singing man in the bin, Millie said goodbye to her friend and ended the call.

'Everything okay?' Floyd asked.

'Yes, thank you. That was Maddie, who has wanted to kill you at times,' Millie told Floyd.

Floyd frowned. 'I can understand. I really hurt you, didn't I?' he said.

'Yes, you did. I thought we were over, and I had no idea why,' Millie confirmed, arms folded across her chest.

'Never, Millie. I know I love you, I always will, and I'm so sorry that for a while, *you* didn't know that. I got so caught up in our future that I didn't think about how you'd be feeling in the present,' Floyd replied.

Every time Floyd told Millie he loved her, it melted away some of her crossness and sadness. He really did sound sorry. If asked, she couldn't have said what made her believe and forgive him. It had something to do with the sorrow in his tone and the softness in his brown eyes, but she couldn't quite put her finger on it.

'Shall we hug it out?' Millie asked.

'Yes, absolutely! I'm never going to say no to a hug from you,' Floyd agreed.

The crowds of people on King's Parade were too busy watching a man busk in a bin or focusing on getting from A to B to notice a happy couple hugging. The busker's music and distant conversations drowned out the couple's declarations of love to each other. They were in their own little world in the middle of a busy city.

When in Floyd's presence, Millie was often only aware of him. Her surroundings faded into the background. This was especially true when she hugged him. As their embrace ended though, Millie was acutely aware she and Floyd were in the middle of Cambridge and had walked a strange route to get there. Their destination was a mystery to her.

'Where are we heading to?' Millie asked.

'Landing Stage. I think it's near Jesus Green,' Floyd told Millie.

Millie grinned. 'That's about half a mile away. We're going punting then,' she said.

'I couldn't possibly say. It's a surprise,' Floyd replied.

43

Chapter Forty-three

As Millie had suspected, they were punting. Floyd had pre-arranged it, goodness knows when. Josh, their chauffeur and tour guide, watched with a smile as Floyd helped Millie onto the boat. He then gave Floyd a blanket, which Floyd wrapped round him and Millie. She snuggled closer once covered by the blanket.

Once his passengers were sat comfortably, Josh began to guide the boat along the River Cam.

'I can't believe you've arranged all this! A house move and this wonderful treat,' Millie cried.

'You're special, and I want you to feel it. Besides, you know how much I love being romantic,' Floyd replied.

'I do, although please never be quite so secretive again,' Millie said.

'I promise you I won't be,' Floyd told Millie.

As the punt approached a bridge, Josh cleared his throat. 'This is Magdalene Bridge,' he told the happy couple on board.

Even though it wasn't the most interesting river crossing, Millie and Floyd admired Magdalene Bridge in reverent silence.

It excited Millie to be on a punt travelling along the route known as "The Backs". It was a very touristy thing to do. As she was a student in the city and poor, Millie had never been on a punt down the Cam, or any river.

'Now this beauty up ahead is The Bridge of Sighs. It is said that any couple who kisses underneath it will enjoy everlasting love. That is a legend about The Bridge of Sighs in Venice, and this one is in Cambridge and officially called New Bridge, but I think it will work for you two,' Josh said.

On the approach to it, Millie and Floyd gazed up at the gothic structure spanning the river. Unlike the previous bridge, this one was covered and had grand but glassless windows.

As they passed under The Bridge of Sighs, Millie and Floyd shared a kiss that warmed them up on the chilly January day.

'There. Eternal love sorted,' Millie declared.

As Floyd agreed, he smiled at the women he was to share eternal love with.

-

For many minutes, Millie and Floyd sat quietly, holding hands under their blanket, listening to Josh give them facts about the various bridges and colleges they passed. She kept thinking about how incredible it was that Floyd had arranged so much, all for her.

When Josh told his passengers the next bridge was King's College Bridge, designed by William Wilkins, Millie thought of yet another thing Floyd had done for her. 'To move to Waterbeach, you must have changed jobs,' she realised aloud.

As Millie was admiring Trinity Hall, she didn't see Josh smile at the mention of Waterbeach.

'Yes, I've changed jobs. The network I used to work for have bought out a smaller MVNO, who have offices and a call centre just outside Cambridge. This Cambridge network need new staff, including supervisors. I applied for complaints supervisor, and, thanks to a good word from my old supervisor back in Colchester, I got it. I found out I'd been successful the day we shared hot chocolate in Castle Park. You very nearly rumbled me thanks to the text flashing up on my watch, but thankfully I dealt with it,' Floyd revealed.

'Wow. You really have done so much! How sneaky but loving you are!' Millie cried.

'Thanks, I think,' Floyd replied.

The punt drifted under a bridge thanks to the expert guidance of Josh. The towering gothic splendour of King's College Chapel then came into view.

'This, sir, is King's College Chapel,' Josh told Floyd.

'I study behind there. This is my educational home,' Millie commented.

Floyd placed a finger on Millie's lips, prompting her to fall silent. Their eyes locked. Neither of them were aware the boat had stopped, even though one of them had asked for the trip to pause there when he'd arranged it.

'These last few weeks have been the happiest of my life. Christmas usually is a good time for me, but this year it was even more special. I was gifted something precious, something I've searched for my whole adult life. You gave me love, Millie. Clever and cute as you are, with your curvy and womanly body, sparkling eyes, and lovely laugh, I couldn't help but fall for you, even though you are my best friend's sister,' Floyd told Millie.

As he was still gazing into them, Floyd could see Millie's eyes were brimming with tears. She now knew what his biggest surprise was going to be.

For countless nights, Floyd had laid awake in the early hours planning this moment. Now the time had come, the words he'd so carefully chosen evaded him.

'Ask me, Floyd. Please ask me. I know we've only been together for a short while, but I'll say yes. I know you're not Prince Hans,' Millie begged.

It didn't matter what Floyd said. He already had what he wanted. The girl he loved had given her agreement to be with him for the rest of their lives. She had also, in typically adorable Millie fashion, made a *Frozen* reference. It was so like her, it warmed Floyd's heart, and it reminded him why he wanted to ask the question she was going to say yes to.

After a deep breath to steady himself, Floyd went on. 'I never again want you to doubt that I love you. I never again want to be parted from you. It is my greatest wish that we spend the rest of our lives together. You're The One,' he said.

From under the blanket, Floyd produced a small box. He sprung it open to reveal a silver ring. The heart cut clear stone in the centre sparkled in the weak winter sun, but not as brightly as Millie's eyes. 'Emily Cassandra Austen, my loveable Millie, will you marry me?' he asked.

Millie took the ring from the box and slipped it onto the fourth finger of her left hand. She twisted her hand to catch the light in the stone.

'Is that a yes?' Floyd questioned.

'Of course! I want the pretty ring!' Millie replied.

'It's not a diamond. It's just cubic zirconia,' Floyd pointed out.

Holding Floyd's hand with the one she'd put his engagement ring on, Millie told him: 'They are perfect. Cubic zirconia is for people who need shine but not status, like us. You can buy me a diamond ring on our sixtieth anniversary. We don't need them now. What we have is more precious than anything you can buy.'

Acknowledgements

Thank you to all the wonderful people who read and reviewed The Christmas Genie's Wish. The support and love you gave Eugenie's story inspired me to write a second Christmas romance novel. It was every bit as enjoyable as the first.

Mum is the biggest champion of my books. I have so much to thank her for. In this I shall thank her for providing endless encouragement and ideas when I struggled to work out what my characters wanted to do in this story.
Another source of bookish support is the unique and kind online collective of people that is Heidi Swain and Friends - A Facebook Book Club. Sue and Fiona work tirelessly to run it and I know I'm not the only author who appreciates all they do for us. The friends part of the group's title is very accurate. There are few times I feel less lonely than when I'm scrolling through the group.
A few members of the Heidi Swain and Friends group contributed to this book. Maddie is named after Miriam O'Brien's puppy. Claire Rowland provided the excellent word confuzzled for Millie to say. When asked to name a venue, Pam Constable suggested a concert at Edinburgh Castle. The ribbon chains Millie buys her parents are inspired

by chains Josie Knight makes. She has a Facebook page called Josies Crafts.
When I need a little inspiration or some finer details, I often look online. For their websites that helped me, I'd like to thank Google, Prestige Flowers, University of Cambridge, UCAS, ABC, BrainyQuote, Tampax, Yours Clothing, ASDA, National Rail Enquiries, Firstsite, Mrs Salisbury's of Maldon, GreyFriars Colchester, BBC Good Food, Visit Buckinghamshire, Ark Cambridge, Manchester Evening News, Good Housekeeping, Amazon, Cambridgeshire Live, Zoopla, Rutherford's Punting, and Let's Go Punting.
Some inspiration also comes from television. Thank you to Susan Calman and everyone who works on her show Grand Day Out. It is entertaining, uplifting, and it visited Brill Windmill. I would like to apologise to Susan Calman for stealing her "brilliant" joke.

Special thanks to Tru, who always reads my books even though they aren't her usual genre and gives me her honest opinion of them. It's brave, thoughtful, and much appreciated, just like the lady herself (and yes, Tru, I did smile at the fact I've called you a lady). She's even introduced her mother to my books.

Last but not least, thanks to you for reading this. There wouldn't be any acknowledgements to read if people like you didn't keep buying my books.

Other Books By Michaela Trueman

Cue Romance

Their eyes meet across a snooker table… or so Jude thought. In reality, Cecilia, the stunning blonde who's caught his eye is looking at the ball she wants to pot. She hasn't even noticed Jude, but he's noticed her. Cue Romance is a tale of fun, friendship, and love under a mostly-sunny and sometimes seagull-filled Essex sky.

The Christmas Genie's Wish

When a friendly and dedicated person, with a creative mind and a good knowledge of the local businesses and their stock and services is required to fulfill the role of Christmas Genie (a personal shopper with a less dull title), there's just one girl for the job.

All year round, Eugenie Holland dresses up the people of Colchester in the contemporary clothes that her aunt's boutique stocks. Putting a smile on customer's faces puts a smile on hers. This makes her the perfect person to be The Christmas Genie.

While helping other people buy presents, The Christmas Genie herself finds the very thing she wants for Christmas. He ticks every box of her wishlist, but will he be present on Christmas Day?

Home Is Where the Heart Is

After her relationship with Shaun, a man who she thought was dependable and honest, comes to a shocking end, Mackenzie Wight's world changes completely. Sheffield, her beloved hometown, is suddenly full of reminders of a man she's now desperately trying to forget.

When Mackenzie is given an excuse to live with her recently-divorced granddad in Colchester, a small town hundreds of miles from home that she's never been to before, she jumps at the chance to escape and make a fresh start.

Though Mackenzie intends to stay single and keep life simple for a while, those around her have other ideas. Things in Colchester get complicated, and moving location hasn't moved her mind on. Can she build a new life for herself, or will change prove impossible?

Fool Me Thrice

Whilst queueing in the supermarket to buy ingredients to cook a special dinner for her gorgeous long-term boyfriend, Ronnie, Emma-Leigh sees an advert for a blind dating event inspired by her favourite TV show. As she is already very much in love, she scrolls past it. A few hours later, she finds her beloved in bed with another woman. The friend she stays the night with convinces the unexpectedly newly-single Emma-Leigh to sign up for the dating event whilst watching the show it was inspired by with her.

The very thought of Ronnie, makes Emma-Leigh sick, let alone the idea of sharing a house with him, so she returns to the village where she grew up. There she finds squabbling sisters, a disapproving mother, and a long list of household tasks to complete in lieu of rent. Geographically, Writtle is more than twenty miles from Ronnie and her life with him, but moving on mentally is as hard as commuting along the busy A12 every day for work.

The experience she's had leaves Emma-Leigh believing she cannot trust any man and will never fall in love again. Can anyone challenge this view and prove her wrong, or will her spirits remain as damp as the autumn leaves that cover the paths of Hylands Park?

Social Media

I like to interact with my fellow readers and writers. If you like giveaways, have any pictures with my books, want to stay up to date with my writing and I, or have any comments to make, please get in touch. I can be found on Facebook and Instagram.

LIKE AND FOLLOW MY FACEBOOK PAGE,
MICHAELA TRUEMAN - AUTHOR.

FOLLOW ME ON INSTAGRAM
@MICHAELA_TRUEMAN_AUTHOR

I'm also on Goodreads and Amazon's Author Central. If you enjoyed reading this book, or even if you didn't, please, please, please leave a review on Amazon or Goodreads. Positive or negative, long or short, reviews help me, and your fellow readers

Excerpt

Here's an excerpt from The Christmas Genie's Wish, my first Christmas novel.

'Oh my, it's you! How *dare* you show your face in here?!' Victoria replied.

The anger in Victoria's voice caught Eugenie's attention. Wanting to see who had angered Victoria so much with their mere presence, Eugenie edged her way to a point where she could just about see out onto the shop floor. All she saw was a customer with no hair who looked to be of around Victoria's age. He didn't look threatening.

'I want to see Eugenie. I want to see my daughter,' the customer told Victoria.

The revelation that the customer was her father froze Eugenie. She wasn't sure whether to run out and introduce herself to the man she'd wondered about all her life, or run away from the man who'd abandoned her pregnant mother.

Victoria scoffed. 'Your *daughter*? You have no right to call her that. You have no right to be here either. Get out, Jason! Do you think, after what you did to my sister, that I'll let you hurt my niece too?' she snapped.

Never before had Eugenie seen a face as disappointed as Jason's when Victoria refused to help. It brought a lump to her throat.

'I was so young. When Liz told me, I was terrified,' Jason said.

'Don't talk to *me* about being scared. I was *Elizabeth's* birth partner. That day, in the delivery room, I saw what fear truly looks like. *You* caused that, and then you didn't stick around to help. Don't you stick around *now*. It's too late. *Now*, you *should* run away, before I call the police to have you removed,' Victoria ranted.

A single tear rolled down Jason's cheek. When she saw it, Eugenie moved to where she could be seen.

When Victoria saw Eugenie out of the corner of her eye, she put a hand out to stop her getting to Jason, or Jason getting to her.

'Eugenie, my daughter! I'm Jason, your dad. Well, the man who got your mum pregnant. I suppose I don't suppose I deserve the title of "dad". I wanted you to know who I am. I wanted to see you. Your aunt won't let me stay though, so I must go. At least I got to see how beautiful you've become,' Jason called to Eugenie.

The lump in Eugenie's throat got bigger as she listened to the first words her father had ever said to her. It prevented her from answering.

'Out!' Victoria barked.

Jason was turning to leave before Victoria shouted at him. All her one word did was speed him up.

When Victoria caught the look in Eugenie's eyes as they both watched Jason leave, she knew exactly what she was thinking. 'Don't. He's scum. Just think of the situation he left your mother in,' she said.

'But he's my father,' Eugenie replied.

Slipping past her aunt's arm, Eugenie dashed out of the shop.

Once out on the icy bricks of the Lane outside Toothill's, Eugenie couldn't run.

As he was in trainers, not high heels, and he cared less about safety than Eugenie did, Jason *could* run.

To stop Jason running back out of her life, Eugenie called: 'Father! It's me, Eugenie! Wait!'

The words echoing off the buildings were exactly the ones Jason had hoped for. They caused him to stop and turn around.

Across the cold grey bricks of the Lanes, Eugenie took the few steps that separated her from her father.

'Why now?' Eugenie asked, as it was the first question that popped into her head.

Ingram Content Group UK Ltd.
Milton Keynes UK
UKHW021430300623
424349UK00014B/397